MY LIFE ON A DIET

MY LIFE ON A DIET

Confessions of a Hollywood Diet Junkie

RENÉE TAYLOR

G. P. PUTNAM'S SONS
New York

G. P. Putnam's Sons
Publishers Since 1838
200 Madison Avenue
New York, NY 10016

Copyright © 1986 by Renée Taylor
All rights reserved. This book, or parts thereof,
may not be reproduced in any form without permission.
Published simultaneously in Canada by
General Publishing Co. Limited, Toronto

Typeset by Fisher Composition, Inc.

Library of Congress Cataloging-in-Publication Data
Taylor, Renée.
My life on a diet.
1. Taylor, Renée 2. Actors—United States—
Biography. 3. Dieters—United States—Biography.
I. Title.
PN2287.T18A3 1986   792'.028'0924 [B]   86-17003
ISBN 0-399-13205-8

Printed in the United States of America
1 2 3 4 5 6 7 8 9 10

*To Phil Stutz, for encouraging me
to write this book.*
AND
*To Joe Bologna, my "boyfriend,"
for loving my talent
and not being jealous that I dedicated
this book to Phil Stutz.*

ACKNOWLEDGMENTS

I am very grateful to Body by Jake and Pete Steinfeld, for recreating my body as a size 4 for me, and to the following people for bringing love and magic to my life, and believing in my talent:

    Frieda Silverstein   Richard Robertiello
    Charles Wexler   Elaine May
    Beverly Dennis   Maria Bernstein
    Dan Casriel   Oliver Hailey

And George Abbott, Bella Abzug, Martin Abzug, Goodman Ace, Louise Adamo, Dick Adler, Buddy Allen, Steve Allen, Woody Allen, Carmel Altomare, Vinnie Altomare, Irv Arthur, Larry Auerback, Mary Jean Badalementi, Clive Barnes, Joanne Baron, Marty Baum, Frank Baxter, Bob Bean, Stuart Berger, Jeanne Berlin, Bobby Bernard, Joey Bishop, Barbara Bologna, Josie Bologna, Tony Bologna, Ed Bondy, Tex Bovary, Marty Bregman, Mel Brooks, David Brown, Georgia Brown, Jay Burton, John Cassavetes, Harris Cattleman, Carol Channing, Robert Chartoff, Nancy Lee Cheeks, Harold Clurman, James Coco, Sam Cohen, Joan Collins, Perry Como, Jimmy Cota, Warren Cowan, Joan Crawford, Judith Crist, Michael Dare, Tomm Dedini, Marlene Dietrich, Barry Diller, Phil Donahue, Phillip V. Dougherty, Hugh Downs,

ACKNOWLEDGMENTS

Bobby Drivas, Bernice Edelman, Charlie Edelman, Peter Falk, Shera Falk, Clay Felker, Jane Fonda, Bob Fosse, Nick Frangakis, Gerald Franklin, Tony Garafolo, Roy Gerber, William Gibson, Bob Goldfarb, Jeanne Goldfarb, Charlotte Goldwasser, Betty Grable, Virginia Graham, Al Greco, Ann Greco, Roger Greenspan, Merv Griffin, Charles Grodin, Helen Gurley Brown, Bill Haber, Elizabeth Forsythe Hailey, Bill Hickey, Ruth Horne, Ray Katz, Dorriett Kavanaugh, Carol Kellner, Jerry Kennealy, Bruce Kirby, John Kirby, Allen Klein, Ron Konecky, Jerry Kramer, Terry Landeck, Floria Lasky, Louise Lasser, Irving Lazar, Frank Leberman, Michele Lee, Fred Levinson, Arthur Levy, Barbara Levy, Jerry Lewis, Moss Mabry, Shelley Maibaum, Ed Marinaro, Carol Matthau, Walter Matthau, Judy Mazel, Vaughn Meader, Jayne Meadows, Marty Melzer, Nancy Melzer, David Merrick, Ellen Meyers, Ron Meyers, Marilyn Monroe, Monty Morgan, Catherine Moyers, Abe Newborn, Mike Nichols, Robert Osborne, Glyn Owen, Jack Paar, Joe Papp, Molly Picon, Kevin Pine, Letty Pogrebin, Peggy Pope, Tom Poston, Morrie Pynoos, Rita Pynoos, Peter Rainer, Bea Rendino, Joe Rendino, Burt Reynolds, Pat Rico, Isabel Robbins, Gail Rock, David Rubenfine, Barbara Rush, Gloria Safier, Gene Saks, Julian Schlossberg, Aaron Schwab, Fay Schwab, Ann Shanks, Bob Shanks, Martin Sheen, Rod Sheldon, Michael Sherman, Fred Silverman, Neil Simon, Frank Sinatra, Ralph Stantley, Gloria Steinem, Anna Strasberg, Lee Strasberg, Barbra Streisand, Kevin Thomas, Marlo Thomas, Brenda Vaccaro, Dick Van Patten, Patty Van Patten, Mike Wallace, Barbara Walters, Richard Watts, Arthur Weiner, Jerry Weintraub, Dr. Ruth Westheimer, Barbara Wexler, Bernard Wexler, Celia Wexler, Myrna Wexler, George White, Gene Wilder, Esther Williams, Barry Wolf, Joan Worth, Marvin Worth, and Richard Zanuck.

And special thanks to Lazaris for teaching me how to unlock my joy. And to Jach Purcell and Penny Prestini for sharing Lazaris with me and the rest of the world.

CONTENTS

	A Loving Warning	11
	INTRODUCTION: WHO AM I?	13
1.	BABY FAT	17
2.	YOUNG FAT	29
3.	CAREER GIRL FAT	41
4.	A LITTLE OLDER FAT	66
5.	MARRIED FAT	82
6.	BEVERLY HILLS FAT	99
7.	DESPERATION DIETING	112
8.	BROADWAY LULLABY, HOLLYWOOD SONATA	131
9.	OVEREATERS ANONYMOUS	144
10.	THE OTHER WOMAN	155
11.	LEAN AND SERENE AT LAST	171
12.	THE TAYLOR-MADE DIET	184

Nobody ever died of starvation from not eating between meals.
—*Overeaters Anonymous Saying*

A Loving Warning

This book includes a diet. Don't go on the diet, or any diet, until you have had a medical checkup, or you can make yourself sick. If you are under a doctor's care for any medical condition, you must have your doctor supervise your diet. This diet is not intended for and should not be followed by people with diabetes, hypoglycemia, heart disease, gastrointestinal problems (including spastic colon or colitis), or by pregnant women or nursing mothers.

INTRODUCTION: WHO AM I?

When I was a young girl growing up I dreamed of leading a glamorous life and having everything a person could ever want: money, success, fame. Yet no one was more surprised than I was that my wishes came true in every way. I grew up to be an actress and a writer, nominated for an Academy Award, winner of an Emmy and Writers Guild Award. I am the president of Taylor-Bologna Productions, a company consisting of me and the man I have been happily married to for twenty years, my partner and collaborator, Joseph Bologna. We have a seventeen-year-old son, Gabriel, who goes to Beverly Hills High School and is just beginning his acting career. We live in a large English Tudor–style house, and we have two secretaries and two housekeepers—two because there is so much activity in our house from all the projects we are working on and the friends and family who come to visit us. I joke about our running the busiest hotel on our block in Beverly Hills.

My world was so full of all the good things in life that my cup had runneth over and so had my appetite.

As a fatty, I was (and still am) under constant pressure in my life; at work, at play, and as a hostess—another role I'm called upon to play in a grand style. I recently gave a charity dinner party for 250 guests at the last minute because the people who had pledged to do it in their home got a job out of town and had to take it because they needed the money to be able to make a donation!

I'm not going to blame my crazy lifestyle for my having been fat even though a lot of people would. In show business the stakes are so high, the risks so great, that many people crack from the strain.

It's very interesting that only *after* I married and my love life became satisfying, and *after* my career was fulfilling, did I start to get really fat. Perhaps I was afraid that I didn't deserve all this good fortune and I overate to compensate for my fear of losing it. Whatever the reason, I finally decided to get my thinness back first and find out why I'd lost it later. This book is about my odyssey to thindom and how I discovered the diet that helped me to recapture my favorite figure—for good!

I want to share what I learned with you and to reaffirm my commitment to myself to be thin, because being thin is easy now. Being thin makes me proud of myself because I look better and I feel better and sexier. I never wanted my picture taken in Hollywood when I was heavy. I had to beg off being photographed beside Morgan Fairchild because I didn't want to be compared to a thin star. Now, I'll run up to Joan Collins and stand next to her because I want to show off how I look.

When I was fat, I read all the diet books as soon as they were printed, and I tried all the diets. They were mostly written by doctors, nutritionists and psychiatrists. I am none of those things. I am only qualified to write this book because I am a former full-time fatty and an expert on being crazy and desperate in an affluent and erratic lifestyle. Luckily, when I was the fattest I've ever been and looked the most bloated I found this way to eat and be very merry on my Taylor-Made Diet.

I wasn't born fat but started to gain weight shortly after my sixth birthday. I stayed that way until last year during my mid-life crisis, when I suddenly figured out how to lose weight on a diet of my own making. I had been on every popular diet of the time since I was eleven years old and had tried all the exercise programs.

I have been to spas around the world, and I have heard what the foremost authorities on diet, health, exercise, eating disorders, nutrition and hypnotism have to say about weight loss: "You must eat grains in the morning." "You cannot have more than three fruits a day." "You cannot mix cucumber and pineapple." "You can mix anything on an empty stomach." Etc., etc. Nothing worked permanently for me, so I became convinced they all know nothing.

I was so desperate to lose weight that I started researching the history of weight reduction in the United States and thinking about my own history and how my family and the many movie stars who were my beauty role-models have influenced me and my eating habits, as have our world leaders.

Bella Abzug became a friend of mine when she was running for Congress the first time in New York. She was a guiding light of the women's movement. She traveled to all the world conferences. Whenever she returned I'd ask her what everyone ate. I began forming my theory that there's a direct correlation between what the heads of countries eat and how aggressive or peaceful their behavior and that of their nations' people is. Hence, I believe sugar, salted foods, chemicals, preservatives, processed foods and excessive fats, meats and dairy products cause people to behave illogically, irrationally and sometimes violently. For instance, Gaddafi is very big on pigs' brains and intestines and salted date balls. Gorbachev lives on lamb balls in chicken fat and bakalah in thick cherry syrup. On the other hand, I have found that men in the peace movement who were strict low-salt vegetarians were hostile to women. So I came to the conclusion that mineral and vitamin deficiencies can make you "nuts" as well.

Since I was a child, I have had total recall about what everybody was eating just before, during and after practically every experience I had. I guess it was part of my ongoing life's investigation of the answer to these questions: Why had I been fat for more than half of my life? How important was my thinness to me? Where did my appetite come from? What could I do to stop bingeing? How could I stay thin for the rest of my life? And, what was causing me to overeat?

In trying to answer these questions, I discovered a secret that made me so happy that I had to write this book.

I had spent my whole life being on a diet, and all I ever thought about was what I was going to eat when I got *off*. That's why all diets fail, because the moment the dieter feels deprived, eating gets out of control. That's how I discovered my Taylor-Made way of eating. It's the diet that you won't cheat on because it allows you to eat everything you are fantasizing about. I even start it on Tuesday, so that on Monday, traditionally the first day for starting new diets, you can fail at whatever diet plan you try before starting mine. That way your failing is already out of the way.

My diet plan is like sex: You can't get too much of it when it's your own creation, not someone else's. You'll choose your favorite starch—rice, potatoes or spaghetti—and you can have it all day. Or you can choose your favorite dessert, and you can have it all day. Or protein—fish, meat, veal or a chicken dish—all day. Or fruit, or salad. You don't feel deprived, you don't feel guilty, and so you're in control of your weight.

And when you can eat all you want of the one thing you want, you'll see you won't want it that much, or that much *of* it. The Taylor-Made Diet is the most fun you can have eating without being arrested. After all those years of being part of the 20 percent of the population who flip back and forth between dieting and bingeing, I have finally taken the weight off for good. Here's my story—I hope it will help you, too, to be thin for life!

1
BABY FAT

I come from a family of Russian Jews who emigrated to this country in flight from the Cossacks. It seemed to me that in our food preparation and dietary habits we were still fleeing, if not the Russian police, somebody. I remember my father, Charlie Wexler, at mealtimes, eating standing up at the end of the table with his hat on. He was either running off to work or else he had just come home and had a "few minutes" before he'd be out the door again.

Charlie Wexler's Diet

Breakfast: Salami and eggs
Orange juice
Bagel
Lunch: Burned steak on a hard roll with tomatoes
Dinner: Flanken (soup meat)
Potato pancakes
Kasha vanakas (kasha and noodles)
Applesauce

This was a "working-man's" diet in 1932. He died at age forty-two, a victim of a heart attack and a broken heart that he couldn't crack the American Dream. He had too much fat and cholesterol in his body. He smoked three packs of unfiltered cigarettes a day, worked eight hours lifting boxes, played cards till all hours, hoping to get "lucky," and slept less than four hours a night.

He called himself a "weatherman." He would look out the window and, depending on the weather, he'd decide what he would sell on the avenue that day. Umbrellas in the rain, oranges in the heat, balloons at a parade, etc. He was a very good-looking man whose considerable charm and humor with the ladies more than made up for his lack of any formal education. At seven, he was out on the street working with his brothers to support his sisters and his mother.

His mother, Yetta Wexler, lost her husband, Borah, to dysentery just before she boarded the boat to America, nine months pregnant. She gave birth to Charlie on the boat coming over to this country with her seven other children. In Russia, she had worked in the potato fields of Borah's farm. The day she gave birth to her daughter Bea in the fields, she resumed plowing immediately afterward. She was senile when she died at eighty, in the Bronx, of hardening of the arteries.

Yetta Wexler's Diet

Breakfast: Lox, eggs and a bagel
Lunch: Borscht with sour cream and a potato
Dinner: Chicken soup with chicken matzo balls

Charlie went to Hollywood to seek his fame and fortune when he was twenty-four. He had a photograph taken of himself in a photographer's studio, wearing fur chaps and a cowboy hat, and sent it in to a film company, hoping to appear in a Tom Mix movie. He had a heavy Russian accent, but he thought his chances were good because it was a silent movie. And his family had made such a fuss over his looks! When he didn't get one call in a month, he decided the Heartbreak of Hollywood wasn't for him, and he headed back home to the Bronx, where he soon met my mother at a cousin's birthday party.

She was a beautiful, dark-haired, shy girl named Frieda Silverstein. On their first date, he brought her an umbrella as a gift because it was raining, and a pair of gloves because hers were torn when they had met, and then a bowl of hot soup.

"He was the kindest man I'd ever met," she said. "So I married him."

She also had something else in common with him—a deep yearning to be a star of the silver screen. She often told me that shortly after she met my father, she answered an ad in the paper: D. W. Griffith advertised for "50 Beautiful Girls, 50," auditions at the Biograph Studios in the Bronx. She got all dressed up, took the day off from the laundry where she worked, and boarded the Tremont Avenue subway to go to the audition. When she arrived at the entrance to the film studio, she noticed just how beautiful the other girls were who were already leaving.

"My finger was on the front doorbell, but my nose seemed so big next to the other girls'. In that one fatal moment, I made the decision to give up my career and marry Charlie," my mother said. I always meant to ask her "What career?" But I never did.

Nine months later I was born and she named me after Renée Adorée, her favorite film star from *The Big Parade*. Astrologically, it was predicted at my birth by my horoscope that I was destined to be a great star, and this was corroborated by tarot cards and tea leaves.

Luckily, or unluckily, depending on how you look at it, I was a chubby baby. That allowed my mother to call my obesity baby fat for the first fifteen years.

"Good morning, Miss Sunshine, the world is waiting for you," is the way she awakened me each morning. And I believed her. Once she said, "Go show the neighbors how pretty you look." I ran to the apartment next door and knocked. The neighbor and her twin daughters, my age, all came to the door.

"My mother told me to show you how pretty I look," I said.

When they slammed the door shut in my face, little did I know that it was a sign of things to come.

As early as I can remember, my mother's health was fragile. She was allergic to cold, she said. And we moved from New York to a warmer climate—Miami Beach, Florida—where she became a vegetarian. In those days, a vegetarian was thought to be weird, since meat and potatoes were the healthy, normal diet for the American family.

My mother would exercise on the beach with Bernarr McFadden, a physical culturist who was in his eighties. He celebrated his birthday every year by parachuting from a plane onto the beach, where my mother and many others awaited him for his free exercise classes.

I remember once sitting on the sand next to my mother listening to the lecture Mr. McFadden gave after the exercises, on the evils of meat. The gist of his talk was that animals living on a vegetable diet are strong, but meat-eating animals are ferocious.

I was seven years old, and I felt like a sinner because I loved hot dogs. Whenever my mother couldn't find me she'd go to the delicatessen and catch me eating a frankfurter, bought with twenty-five cents I'd saved.

When Mr. McFadden asked if there were any questions, I raised my hand.

"Do you mean I would be a different girl if I ate a carrot instead of a hot dog?" I asked him.

"Absolutely," said Mr. McFadden. "As the vegetarian said to the cannibal, 'It's not what you eat that counts, it's *who* you eat.'" That was the physical-culture joke of 1941.

The Second World War had just begun, and this is the diet McFadden prescribed for my mother:

Frieda Silverstein Wexler's Diet

Breakfast: Bowl of grapefruit
Lunch: Shredded carrot salad with raisins and apple
Dinner: Broiled fish
Baked potato
Green vegetables

She died, the victim of a heart attack, at the age of sixty-one. (Actually, she was sixty-three. I lied on her death certificate because I thought that would make her happy.) She had only four hours of sleep each night too. She would sit up all night in the bathroom, half of the time crying because my father wasn't home and half of the time reading physical-culture and movie magazines, cutting out the diets of movie stars and famous people of the times and pasting them all over the house.

I never knew which impaired her health more, the crying or the all-night reading. I've always wondered if her last thoughts were of her own unfulfilled hopes or that she was happy that her daughter was on her way to being a movie star. For almost two years after her death, I mourned her—I was afraid the former was true. I was not only at my heaviest weight in those years, I was catatonic. But I'll come to that later.

In Florida, my mother began stuffing me and my brother, Bernard (who was named after a Saint Bernard, so he would be "a friend to man"), out of her terror that if she didn't we would be as sickly as she was. Don't think you can't overeat as a vegetarian, because I did. No one knew about "not mixing foods that don't combine well" then. With Bernard she was always overprotective. Her own brother was shot in a poker game, and she thought that only Bernard's super-health would save him.

Bernard Wexler's Diet

(Measured Portions)

Breakfast: Chicken and eggs on toast
Lunch: Chicken salad
Cottage cheese
Dinner: Broiled chicken
Two vegetables
Baked apple

Her father, Sender, who lived with us, had a raw onion every morning for breakfast, and he attributed his never having a cold to that remedy. Late in the day, he'd chew on a raw garlic clove, and he attributed his physical endurance to that. He was a house painter, and he worked longer hours than the younger men who worked with him. Possibly the fumes he gave off caused everyone to leave the job earlier than he did.

Sender Silverstein's Diet

Breakfast: Raw onion
Lunch: Boiled potato
Raw onion
Sour cream
Dinner: Pot cheese
Boiled potato with sour cream and chives

(Notice the lack of fruit and meat in his diet, but he got his vitamin C from the onions.)

Unknowingly, he was on the longevity diet of the Hunza mountain people in Tibet. He was never sick a day in his life, and he died at seventy-seven, the victim of a hit-and-run driver, his body thrown into the East River.

My mother entertained the soldiers in Flamingo Park by reading their palms. She invited some of them home for Sunday dinner. It was all very innocent at first. "Don't ration your appetite," my mother would tell them, serving them "patriotic foods," which were foods our country and our refrigerator had a surplus of. "Here's to victory," she'd say, holding up a combination of orange, grapefruit and pineapple.

She had beautiful legs that she kept in shape by doing her leg raises, "personally prescribed" by Sylvia of Hollywood. Sylvia was the most famous masseuse and beauty culturist to the stars. Or so said *Photoplay* magazine about her. Each month my mother would send her a dollar and a question about a beauty problem, and Sylvia would answer with an exercise or a health tip.

At the U.S.O., where my mother volunteered to do her part for the war effort, she taught some of the soldiers one of Sylvia's remedies for "nerves."

"Press hard with both your thumbs at the hairline, about an inch from the ears at the back of the head. Dig in deep under the bone. Do this ten times and you'll lose your jitters." My mother would demonstrate, and the soldiers took it all very seriously.

My father was very rarely home. He did such wheelings and dealings with oranges as you wouldn't have believed possible. Because there was such a demand for them, he bought up cheap green oranges off the trees and then ripened them in a room with gas heaters. Eventually, he bought an orange grove that was having trouble with fruit flies. He saved himself money by not taking out hurricane insurance, because it was expensive and "What are the odds there will ever be a hurricane—a million to one?" Of course, there was a hurricane, and he was wiped out—one of the many "unlucky" circumstances that happened to him again and again.

Meanwhile, my mother was getting a lot of attention for herself from our boys in the service. She became known as a naturopath. That's when she met Sam. I don't remember his last name—only that he was a soldier, very fair and sensitive looking, and I could tell from the beginning he was in love with my mother. "He's a fruitatarian," my mother would say about him wistfully, as though that was the finest thing you could say about a man. "He eats only things that fall from a tree or grow in the ground." Nuts, fruits, and berries, and spaghetti and rice. At the canteen, she would sit and watch him eat for an hour at a time. I watched her watching him. He was practicing Fletcherism, the belief started by Horace Fletcher that through chewing the food until it liquefies, the digestion was aided. I tried it once and almost got lockjaw. Several months afterward, Sam was shipped overseas. I could tell my mother thought about him a lot at night, as she watched my father the meat eater standing up at the table with his hat on, eating his flanken, chewing hardly at all.

Miami Beach was the promised land to my father's brothers and sisters. One by one they announced they were coming for a winter visit. They had to sleep on the couch in the dining room because my grandfather slept in the living room and we only had a small two-bedroom apartment. It had one bedroom for me and my three-year-old brother and one bedroom for my parents.

Those were the days of the War Bond tours, and a lot of stars came from California to appear in them. I sold twenty-five bonds for $18.75 each, going door to door, and with each bond came two tickets to the Victory show—one for the bond buyer and one for the seller, me. I sold enough bonds to take my whole family to the shows. We saw Joan Crawford and Clark Gable. After the show, we went backstage. My father and I thought my mother wanted an autograph, but she introduced herself to Joan Crawford as a "friend" of Sylvia, and to our great surprise, Joan Crawford was interested in what my mother had to say.

"Joan," my mother said to Miss Crawford, "I hear you order two slices of raisin bread in the MGM commissary and then pluck out the raisins from the whole-wheat bread and eat them one at a time."

"Yes, I do," Joan said guiltily. "But Sylvia told me to eat plenty of raisins because I need more iron."

"Of course you do," my mother said. "But your body needs whole-wheat bread to keep you constipation-free."

Miss Crawford seemed stunned. "How did you know?" she asked my mother.

"They don't call me 'Frieda, the Psychic Herbologist' for nothing," she said.

"Do you have a card?" Miss Crawford asked.

"No, but here's my phone number," my mother said, writing it down on a piece of paper. "Call me the next time your thighs ache from dancing. I'll give you an exercise. I sense you have trouble with your feet, all the way up, front and back."

It was my mother's moment of triumph. All the years of exercising with Bernarr McFadden and writing to Sylvia had paid off in her being a maven. Next we moved on to Clark Gable's dressing room.

"Clark," my mother said. "I'm Frieda, a friend of Sylvia of *Photoplay*. You always carry pockets full of peanuts, and your favorite sandwich is bacon, Swiss and minced eggs."

"You have me down to a T," Mr. Gable said.

"Well, I want to commend you," my mother said. "Peanuts are a wonder food and your multi-protein sandwich is rich in inositol, which spawns virility."

"I'm glad to hear I'm doing something right," he said, flashing his teeth and walking us to the door.

As we were leaving the Lincoln Theatre stage door, my father said to my mother, "I didn't know you knew so much about foods. Maybe there's a way you could make money from it."

"These psychic insights I have are a gift from God. It would be wrong to make money from them when I'm a mother, because it's a mother's job to be a scientist and have healing powers. Only a few people know the real value of nutrition. You see, Charlie, eating is the one universal attribute of all human beings. Someday, that knowledge will change history and be worth *millions*. Who's going to pay me that now? Besides, Renée's going to be a rich and famous star, and then I'll be asked to publish everything in *Photoplay* magazine too," she said.

After my mother's dissertation, my father and I looked at each other, suspecting my mother was nuts, but we weren't sure.

Meanwhile, we were broke again. My father had bought watermelons—small ones—very cheap. With a bicycle pump, he filled them up with air to make them larger, since they sold by the pound. Naturally, many of them burst open from the pressure. But my mother saved the day by remembering reading that Jimmy Stewart drank watermelon juice in the service to help his night blindness when he flew a B-29. My father made money selling "Vitamin C Watermelon Juice" to the army mess halls.

Even though my mother asked everyone she ever met whether she should have her nose fixed, I thought her nose was perfect and that she was so beautiful I paled beside her. Once we met a famous plastic surgeon at a bus stop and she asked his professional opinion about how he'd do her nose operation.

"A nose job wouldn't do you or my reputation any good," he said. "So it's got a bump and maybe it's long, but what you've got there is the Romanesque nose of a real beauty," he said.

"I agree," I said, not knowing what a Romanesque nose looked like.

"You have a smart daughter," the surgeon said. "Your looks and her brains could go far."

I was hurt, but I knew it was true. I remember that kicked off my first binge. I began with tuna fish and six slices of white bread. My mother called white bread "the enemy of good health."

My first diet started when I was eleven and a size eighteen. I was overdosing on Wonder bread—a loaf a day.

I had skipped ahead a whole year in school, and I was put in a class with prettier, more developed girls. One day, I was sent home from school because my teacher said I could not go five minutes without a piece of bagel in my mouth. I loved bagels and I still do. Probably that's why I was forced to invent a diet where once in three weeks you can have bagels all day if you choose to, but back then I felt I couldn't compete with my mother's looks or with the other girls at school, so why try?

My mother dragged me from doctor to doctor because I was so fat and getting fatter. She begged them, "Please do something for her. She can't stop eating. I know she has a large frame, but maybe you'll find it's a tapeworm that's causing it. She can't eat just *one* piece of anything, not even a carrot or a piece of celery."

One doctor said I had a sluggish thyroid, and my mother and I were both happy to hear I was "glandular." I took thyroid pills, but I knew it wouldn't help, and it didn't. I knew that the main gland responsible for my overeating was the salivary gland. Until I was fifteen I was built like a large sugar cube—squared off at the corners—and then I fell madly in love. But it wasn't a boy who made me finally lose weight—it was the laughs I heard the first time I walked out on stage in junior high school. I had fallen madly in love with the idea of being an actress.

I knew that I would have to lose weight or I wouldn't be allowed to play leading roles in high school. I tried all the diets that were popular then, even though my mother didn't approve of any of them. I had been a sneaky eater, now I became a sneaky dieter. It was my rebellion.

The Fabulous Formula Diet

Six portions—900 calories. Mix together 10 ounces of dextrose, 10 ounces of evaporated milk, 1 ounce of corn oil and 8 ounces of water. Resembles breast milk.

The Grapefruit Diet

6 grapefruit a day

The Hamburger and Water Diet

16 glasses of water and 6 hamburgers
(The water flushes out the red meat.)

Each diet worked, but then I'd have an emotional injury and I'd get heavy again. For instance, I wanted to quit junior high school and join the circus as a high-wire twirler when Ringling Brothers came to town. My mother said that without a high school diploma no one would ever hire me. And that was a good excuse to overeat.

Then, in the middle of my last term, our whole life in Miami Beach fell apart. My father had become a problem gambler.

Maybe it was because he worked so hard on the streets at such a young age. Gambling was his way of being a kid again. The two pieces of jewelry my father gave my mother, a cocktail ring and a matching cocktail watch, he won in a game. When he had a loss, he'd hock them to get back in a game. Sometimes I'd come home from school and want a snack, and the refrigerator was totally bare except for one hard-boiled egg. Then I'd know he was on a losing streak. Sometimes the refrigerator would be filled with salami, cheese and smoked fish, and I'd know he was a big winner. As his fortunes went, so went my weight—in the opposite direction: If he won, my weight went down; if he lost, my weight went up.

My father disappeared for two days. When he came home, he told us he had lost everything we had in a poker game. We piled all of our belongings on his truck and waited until the middle of the night to beat paying the rent. Then we all skipped town. Needless to say, I was a tub. I weighed so much my mother and brother sat up front with my father and I sat on the back of the truck all the way from Miami Beach to New York City.

2
YOUNG FAT

I always wanted to be famous. In the beginning I didn't ask myself: famous for what? Then as a teenager I saw what a serious craft acting was and I became dedicated and discovered the joy of being creative, first as an actress and then a writer. However, very early I yearned to be free from my own ambitions, because I felt I had to share whatever I accomplished with my mother, who lived vicariously through me. It seemed as though she took a back seat to me, but when someone needs you to be famous so they can be too, they are Number One and you are Number Two. What made it worse was that I adored her and I felt her pain. I would have done anything to make her happy, except be thin.

At sixteen I entered the American Academy of Dramatic Arts in New York, and I was really a tub. I had stunned the judges doing the death scene from *Romeo and Juliet* for my audition. I ate a whole raw onion before I went onstage, which doubled me over with tears and made me actually feel like I was dying. That was the only way I knew how to be "real," and without a technique, I didn't want to fake it.

A lot of movie stars sent their children to the academy, and either because of my weight or because I was the daughter of nobodies, I played their maid in a lot of plays.

I had one girlfriend from the academy who was very stuck-up. Her father was a very big film actor. On several occasions I had dinner with my stuck-up girlfriend and her father at their penthouse on Fifth Avenue. After dinner I watched him eat candy corn. First he ate the tip, then he bit off the end part. Last, he savored putting the middle orange part of the candy in his mouth. I was mesmerized.

One night I was on my way to the spring dance at the Thespian Society, an acting club at the academy. I had bought a chartreuse satin off-the-shoulder dress, long black gloves and I was wearing my mother's white fox boa. I rang the bell to pick up my girlfriend, who was more the June Haver wholesome type. She let me in and asked me to keep her father company in the library while she changed. The Ink Spots' recording of "If I Didn't Care" was playing on the phonograph. As I walked up the stairs to the music, I started to become Betty Grable, whom I had seen play opposite my girlfriend's father in an early movie of his.

"Hi, Mr. L.," I said.

"Hello. New dress?" Mr. L. said, putting down the paper.

"Yes," I said. "Don't you think it's kind of sexy?" I asked.

"Now that you mention it, it is sort of," Mr. L. said.

"Uh, Mr. L., would you mind if I played 'Moon Over Miami' after the Ink Spots? I do a little dance to it," I said.

"Sure, go ahead," Mr. L. said.

As I hummed "Moon Over Miami" and shook my body, Mr. L. said, "Gee, you're a natural dancer." His eyes were glazed.

"Think so?" I said.

Mr. L. was starting to perspire.

"What are you thinking about, Mr. L.?" I asked.

I knew what he was thinking. But it was exciting doing repartee with him, like a sex goddess.

"I was thinking, If only I were twenty years younger," Mr. L. said.

"What would you do if you were twenty years younger?" I asked.

"Uh, I would probably put my arms around you," he answered.

And he did.

"And then what would you do, Mr. L.?" I asked.

"And then I would—"

Mr. L. took my face in his hands and kissed me with his mouth open. There was a piece of candy corn in his mouth and he pushed it into mine. I wondered if Betty Grable had ever had that done to her.

"And then I would—"

He lifted up my dress and laid me down on the couch. I didn't ask him "And then what would you do?" because I was busy wondering what the hell I should do with the candy corn in my mouth. I didn't know if I was supposed to put it back in his mouth, or what. And anyway, it was all over in a second and I didn't have time! The phonograph stuck on "Moon Over Miami," as Mr. L. zipped up his pants and whispered, "Did you like it?"

"Oh, I loved it," I said.

"Sorry it was so short. Maybe we can get together like this again soon," he said.

I wanted to say, "We did it already, so what's the point," but I thought it might hurt his feelings, so I said, "Yeah, soon."

I probably never would have seen Mr. L. again if I had liked my girlfriend or if I felt she really liked me, because then I would have felt guilty. But I didn't, so I saw him whenever he wanted to so I could practice my acting on him. We'd go up to his library late at night and do it on his leather couch. He had a lot of popularity awards on the walls, and once the thrill of the candy corn in my mouth was over, I read all his awards while he was on top of me. Without any sexual feelings of my own, I imagined what Betty, Lana, Rita and Hedy would be feeling with him. Eventually I got bored with playing these ladies, because they seemed so limited in their facial expressions no matter how hot they got. Just as I didn't understand then that acting is an organic process that comes from within, I didn't know the same was true about sexuality. I was too young to know about my own sexuality, so I faked it. One night as he drove me home, Mr. L. asked me, "Will you think about letting me get you an apartment?"

"It's really not up to me, Mr. L.," I said, getting out of the car. "Since I'm only seventeen, I still live at home. I have a very close relationship with my father, so it's really up to him to decide. But I'll certainly ask him, Mr. L."

A few years later when I did a television show with Betty Grable, I was dying to say to her, "Wasn't it fun what we did to Mr. L.?"

A few weeks after my first sexual experience, my mother came to school to hear the guest speaker, Dame Judith Anderson, talk to us about acting. Afterward, my mother brought me to Dame Judith's dressing room.

"Dame," my mother said. "Frieda," pointing to herself. "Maybe you could do something for my daughter, Renée, who's just starting out."

"Like what?" Judith Anderson said incredulously.

"Give her a push on the way up and some day she'll give you one on the way down." I was very embarrassed, but Judith Anderson was amused.

Years later when I was auditioning for Noël Coward's musical *Sail Away*, my mother was waiting for me at the back of the theater. I sang eight bars, and Noël Coward told me, "Thank you very much."

From the back of the theater I heard my mother say, "That's it? Two thousand dollars for singing lessons and that's it?"

"Who is that?" Noël Coward asked, straining to see the back of the theater.

"Noël," my mother said. "Frieda," pointing to herself. "Why don't you let her finish the song? She gets better as she goes along."

"Madame, I have been in the theater all my life, and I can

see immediately if someone is right or wrong for the show," he said.

"Noël, I've seen your last three shows, and if you think you can see right away, you should have your eyes checked."

I thought I was going to die. Noël Coward was not amused. We were escorted out of the theater.

My mother had all the nerve in the world for me and none for herself.

At the academy I studied fencing, speech, makeup, dance and acting technique. It was wonderful and inspiring, but I had a losing battle with my weight.

I found out the diet of an alumna of the school, Grace Kelly, who was just starting to work as a television actress. One of the boys I dated from the academy was a Philadelphia Main Liner, and he knew her and her family very well. He told me she lived on yogurt and fruit, and she skipped meals. That was unheard of in 1951. When she got married years later, I was "engaged" to the society Philadelphian, and we sent her a wedding gift of a lovely crystal fruit bowl. She sent back a thank-you note on her royal stationery, telling us about how much she liked her new home, the palace. I heard from my boyfriend's parents that she was still skipping meals for her skin and her figure.

I was a real shock for his parents. Maybe that's why he was so madly in love with me. Whenever he brought me home to Philly he got a rise out of them. I wasn't obese, but I was *zaftig*—his nickname for me was "tomato head." His family was piss elegant, and this was their menu for Christmas in 1951:

1951 Philadelphia Society Dinner

Goose pâté—Bologna wrapped around chestnuts
Tom turkey stuffed with sausage
Baked macaroni with American cheese
Candied yams with marshmallows melted on top
Vanilla ice cream with marrons glacés

I never saw so much food in my life, yet the whole family was very thin. I soon figured out that, while I couldn't eat enough, they were all just picking.

At the academy, I did excel in *The Torchbearers* as a heavyweight dowager, Mrs. Pampinelli. I was the talk of the school. When the dean called me in to be evaluated at the end of the term, I was decked out in a glamorous hot-lime dress with a hot-lime veil over my face, and I sat expectantly before him.

"Renée, why don't you get married and have children and come back to the theater late in life? That's when we think you'd have a career as a character actress," he said.

"You mean you're not accepting my $500 for the senior year, Mr. Weitzel?" I asked.

"I'm sorry, Renée," he said. "The school is concentrating on girls who will be playing romantic leads."

"I heard you said the same thing to Katharine Hepburn," I said.

"I hope I'm wrong about you too."

You are wrong, Mr. Weitzel, and I will make you eat your words, I thought as I slammed the door behind me and ran down the stairs sobbing.

I began to live to prove him wrong. I went on the diet of the fifties from the book *Calories Don't Count*, by Dr. Herman Taller. Each day I chewed six magic safflower-oil capsules (called CBC) and ate 65 percent fat on his diet, until Dr. Taller was found guilty on twelve counts of fraud. Then he closed his office and I went off his diet.

I signed up at the American Theatre Wing, with all the veterans coming home from Korea, and I had a dance act with five other girls called "The French Girls." We couldn't dance and we couldn't sing French very well, but since we only worked roadside clubs, like the Highway Casino in Massapequa, Massachusetts, the customers were too bombed to notice.

I sent out blotters and pencils and stickers with my picture, name and phone number on them. I put my stickers in phone booths, theatrical bars and the waiting rooms of all the talent agencies in the city. I was bombarded by calls from perverts and a few outraged casting directors who lectured me for my lack of dignity as an artist. I wanted to say, "I got you to call, didn't I?" But I pretended to be touched by their concern, and I got my first job in a movie.

"How would you like to be in a scene with Tyrone Power?" a casting agent asked.

"No nudity, I hope," I said.

"This is a class picture."

"I wouldn't sleep with him either to be in this picture," I said.

"I didn't ask you to," he answered.

"Okay, just because I'm a romantic lead, people get funny ideas."

"Have you got a gown?" he asked.

"Sure," I lied. "What kind of a part is it?"

"She's a dancer. Be at the Waldorf tomorrow at 6:00 A.M."

I borrowed my aunt's gown that she wore to her son's bar mitzvah. Now I was going to be in a movie with Tyrone Power. I sat up all night writing my Academy Award acceptance speech.

"Members of the Academy, I never dreamed when I accepted the part of the dancer in *The Eddie Duchin Story* that I would even be noticed. The fact that I was is a great tribute to all the little people in the motion picture industry. I would like to thank those who believed in me, like my mother and father, and a special thanks to Ty Power. But most of all, I am indebted to Mr. Weitzel, Dean of the American Academy of Dramatic Arts, who turned me down for the senior year and taught me that the true purpose of rejection is to make me deeper."

I took a cab from the Bronx to the Waldorf Astoria. I couldn't believe the crowd of people gathered around the front of the hotel. Were they waiting for me or Tyrone? The doorman opened the cab door for me, and I gave him my hand, laughing as he helped me out. I looked around for the casting director and called to him, "I'm here."

He nodded to me. "Okay, up to the tower." I followed the rush of people to the tower elevator. Then I noticed all the other women wearing gowns—all ages, shapes and sizes. The elevator door opened at the Tower Ballroom. There must have been thousands of people sitting at tables all over the room.

"Sit anywhere," an assistant director yelled to everyone.

I spotted Tyrone and I wanted to yell, "I love you," but he looked so bored and tired. Then I noticed that sitting close to Tyrone, all blond, gentile and cool, as though she just happened to be in the neighborhood for a visit, was Kim Novak. Oh, God. Why did she have to be in my movie? In my only scene? I borrowed one of the extras' binoculars to get a closer look at her. To find out what she was eating for breakfast. What was she drinking? I couldn't believe it. It looked like hot chocolate with whipped cream and a croissant. How smug of her. A man who seemed to be the director spoke through a megaphone.

"All right, people," he said. "Eddie Duchin has just returned from a triumphant tour of Europe. This is his opening night. He plays his opening number, and when he finishes, you all give him a standing ovation. Okay, let's shoot it," he said.

I wondered how I would stand out in the huge crowd of actors. I would cry more when he played the piano. I would yell "bravo" with more passion. I would love him so much more that the camera would "find" my face and dwell on it, and Tyrone would see me in the rushes and send for me. He would tell the studio, "Drop that cold fish, Kim. The money's on this one." I put my head down on the table and dozed off for what seemed like a moment. I thought I heard music playing and people applauding. A warm feeling flowed through my body when I felt someone poking me.

"You," I heard. "Get up."

"Who, me?" I said, lifting my head up.

"Yes, you," the director called. "What's your name?"

"My name?" I thought: This is it. I'm being discovered. I rose from my seat and said, "Renée Wexler."

"I can't hear you," he yelled.

All eyes turned to get a look at me. I noticed Tyrone and Kim straining to see me too.

"Renée Wexler," I yelled back.

"Renée Wexler," he said, pointing to the exit door, "you're through at Twentieth Century–Fox."

You can see why twenty-five years later making a deal with Twentieth Century–Fox for *Made for Each Other*, with me as the star, was so symbolic. Being humiliated in front of thousands of people at the Waldorf was a good lesson for me—I figured if I could live through that I could take anything.

I had been trying to get in to see a very famous agent for a year. Whenever he heard my name through his office door, I would see his hand with a diamond pinky ring waving me out of the office. One day I told his secretary I wasn't moving unless he came out. I had read there was a part I was right for in the show business newspaper, and I had to be sent by an agent.

"What is it?" the agent asked me, exasperated, as if he was doing me a big favor talking to me.

"The lead in Tennessee Williams' *Baby Doll*. Elia Kazan is seeing only young, voluptuous Southern girls. I'll take speech lessons and perfect a Southern dialect if only you'll get me an interview."

"Okay, kid. I'm going to risk my reputation for integrity for you." He dropped the sandwich he was eating and looked me up and down like I was a cow for sale. I include his diet so you'll know who he is.

Broadway Agent's Diet

Breakfast: Lox, eggs and onion on a hard roll
Lunch: Celery tonic
Hot pastrami on a roll
Coleslaw
Dinner: Egg roll
Spareribs
Fried rice
Chop suey
Pineapple

"But we'd better change your name from Wexler to an authentic old Southern name." He opened the book of *Who's Who in the South*. The only name we recognized was General Rich E. Taylor, and so Renée Taylor was born.

I took speech lessons for a week, bought a merry widow and squeezed up my fat in the middle so it looked like I had a big bosom, a small waist and round hips. I was flabbergasted to meet Tennessee Williams and Elia Kazan. I had barely opened my mouth when Tennessee said, "What part of New York are you from?" So much for my Southern accent, but I kept the name because if "Taylor" had gotten me as far as meeting authentic Hollywood people, there was no telling where I would go from there.

After all these traumatic experiences, I began to feel like a holy person—able to walk through fire and not burn, or eat glass and not get cut. Then one day, when I was auditioning for yet another play, the stage manager asked me, "What part are you here for?"

"My agent said the part where my name goes up over the title," I lied, because the Broadway agent was waving his pinky ring and not seeing me since I lost the *Baby Doll* job.

They handed me the script. I couldn't make heads or tails out of it. That's how I would read, I decided. What worse could happen to me than what happened when I *knew* what I was doing? I was very relaxed. A woman came running onstage after I read only one scene. She said, "You're just what we're looking for. Are you Equity?"

"Oh, sure," I said. "Is this off-Broadway or on?"

"On," she said. "Have you done a lot of Restoration comedy?"

"Oh, yeah," I said, deciding not to ask what it was. "I'll have my agent call you to discuss salary, and don't let him hold you up for a lot of money."

I couldn't believe it. I was nineteen and I had the lead in a Broadway play. I would join Equity and be a Star. The play was called *The Rehearsal* and it was written by George Villiers, the Duke of Buckingham (no less!!), and others—that was the actual author's billing. But first I would go see the Broadway agent who had told me to let him know if I was ever in anything so he could see my work, and now I would floor him with my success.

"My name is going to be above the title. You want to handle the dough?" I asked.

"Sure, how much do you want?" he said, grabbing my hand and putting it over his entire genital area.

"Please, I've only been able to do one thing at a time well," I said, moving my hand away.

"Honey, if you want to play big parts, you have to act like you belong in the theater." He grabbed my hand and put it back on his entire genital area again.

"Tallulah Bankhead said, 'People who play big parts always play with bigger parts,'" I said, patting his genital area before pulling my hand away.

"Tallulah never said that," he said.

"Be sure to get me a minimum contract, and add on a commission for yourself," and I left.

I finally get a big agent interested in me and he turns out to be a creep. I ran home to my parents that night and yelled, "I'm starring on Broadway, and I'm going to be a size eight."

"I knew our day would come," my mother said.

My father said, "They must really be hard up."

In rehearsal I got into a very bad habit. I looked great only when I was acting. I yo-yoed back and forth from a size twelve to my goal of size eight on opening night.

I invited all my old friends from the academy, and I wrote Mr. Weitzel there'd be two tickets for him on opening night, never dreaming he would come to see the girl he turned down for the senior year star on Broadway. I played the part of the playwright's mistress, who performs for the duke and duchess in the play within the play. The audience seemed to be enjoying the play when I made my first entrance on opening night to tremendous applause, and I received an even bigger hand on my first exit. My dressing room was filled with well-wishers. Mr. Weitzel and his wife thanked me for inviting them to a Broadway opening.

"Now you're sorry, I bet, Mr. Weitzel, that I wasn't asked back," I said as he was going out the door, but he laughed without turning back to me.

"How'd you like it, Daddy?" I asked my father, sitting in the corner with his hat still on.

"I like more action," my father said.

"Let's go to Sardi's," the Broadway agent said, grabbing my arm. All evening I hoped he would try to make me touch his genital area again, so I could make a scene now that I was a hit, but he disappointed me. At Sardi's the press agent read the reviews. All terrible, except the *Daily News* said about me, "Renée Taylor, a blonde hoyden, came onstage like she was shot out of a cannon. We should like to see her do something like *Born Yesterday*. She's just the type." The show closed the same night it opened, but it didn't matter. To be praised by the paper with the world's largest circulation was ecstasy. Eight million people would read about me and talk about me. The headlines on the front page were about a huge fire in New Jersey. Even those left homeless by the tragedy would read of my triumph. I imagined a woman standing in the rubble of her home saying to her husband, "When a girl with such talent is picked out, there has to be a God." All week I had dreams of glory about how I would never have to worry again as an actress. But as the months passed, no one called. I couldn't leave the house. I realized what a terrible thing it was to be queen for one day. I couldn't adjust to the other 364 days of the year.

3
CAREER GIRL FAT

The way I bounced back and forth in my weight is the way I bounced back and forth in my career. I tried out as a singer, a dancer, a comedienne, even a show girl when I couldn't get acting work. One time the Broadway agent's cousin, who was a hotel agent, had me work on a comedy act for six months before he booked me in the Catskills. "Get a good report and I'll get you more resort work," he said.

I walked out on the stage of a large bungalow colony. "Good evening, ladies and gentlemen," I said. From the first row I heard a woman announce out loud to the rest of the audience, "Oy, English."

I'd try anything to get acting work. If I auditioned for a commercial and they asked me if I skied, I'd say, "When do you need it by?" My résumé said my age range was thirteen to eighty. I even said my bust range was twenty-two to forty-four. When a casting director asked how that was possible, I said, "I can bind myself down or stuff myself up."

I took turns dressing as different types on different days. I auditioned for a revival of the Ziegfeld Follies at the Winter Garden Theatre on Broadway. The show girls had such big bosoms that I ran into the bathroom and stuffed my red bathing suit with toilet paper. As I went through the paces of the routine, I began to perspire and I watched the toilet paper slowly slide out of my suit. "You," they called to me. "Step forward."

I couldn't believe that they were hiring me. They weren't. One of two hundred girls, I was the first to be eliminated. I realized I was standing next to Julie Newmar, almost 6 feet 3 inches. Naturally, I paled by comparison.

"Could I ask you a personal question?" I said to Julie Newmar on my way out. "What do you eat?"

"Steak tartare," she answered. At that moment, I began my survey of beautiful women, looking for the perfect diet for weight loss. After one day of steak tartare I gained 3 pounds, so that diet was put to bed for all time.

After the American Theatre Wing, I enrolled in Lee Strasberg's acting class, where I remained for eight years as I began to develop my acting technique.

"Are you sure I'm pretty enough to be a movie star?" I continually asked my mother.

"If you want it bad enough, you will be," she'd answer.

"How come *you* weren't able to want it enough to get it for yourself?"

"The last generation didn't have the confidence, the courage, the health or the endurance that this generation has," she answered. Her belief in me was inspiring. With my mother and my father passing me the torch, I felt that there was no question that I would make good. I had to, for all of us.

This omnipotent feeling helped to push me, but it never prepared me for the fact that the world might not agree with my mother's idea of the destiny of Miss Sunshine. One way to get through rejections was not to take being thrown out of offices personally, since these people had not read my horoscope. Another way was simply to endure.

Once I was an extra in the Purim Pageant at Madison Square Garden. I saw Helen Hayes cross herself before she went on. "Miss Hayes, does that help?" I asked her.

"Only if you can act," she answered.

"Go Another Round" was my mother's favorite poem. It

was about a fighter who would never quit a fight. I still think of it when things get tough.

During the eight years in Lee's class, I snuck out and heard what other great acting teachers, like Harold Clurman and Stella Adler, had to say. I saw three psychiatrists at the same time for a year too, because they all saw my weight problem from different angles, and that took off the pressure to solve my career and love dilemmas and my obesity at the same time.

Into Lee's class came some of the most beautiful and famous stars. I met Marilyn Monroe, Jennifer Jones and Joan Crawford, to name a few. From the empty bags, I noticed that Jennifer Jones ate rice cakes and chewed on lecithin.

"What's that do?" I asked her.

"It acts as a fat emulsifier," she said, putting a capsule in my hand. It tasted awful.

Joan Crawford sipped vegetable juice from a can and ate pumpkin seeds by the bag. One day Joan Crawford caught me picking up her seed bag and tin can out of the trash.

"I used to be a garbage eater myself," she said. "Kelp, vinegar and B-6 stabilized me." I was too embarrassed to tell her I wasn't going to eat her food, I just wanted to know what it was.

Joan Crawford's Kelp, Vinegar, B-6 Diet

Keep on a 1000-calorie-a-day regimen. Add 1 teaspoon of cider vinegar three times a day, following each meal. Vitamin B-6 in tablet form is taken three times a day, along with kelp in tablet form, 25 milligrams three times a day.

(Cider vinegar provides potassium and phosphorus. Kelp has thirteen essential elements, including iodine. Fifty milligrams of vitamin B-6 per day acts to combat the effects of stress.)

Marilyn Monroe was, and is to this day, my favorite. I never saw skin like hers—the color of a peach and translucent.

"How did you get skin like that?" I asked her one day in the ladies' room as she put calamine lotion on her face because she was breaking out in a rash. She had just done a scene in class and was so scared her body was dripping wet with perspiration. Her jersey dress stuck to her flesh, and you could see the exact outline of her body through the clinging material. If there was a drop of fat here or there, it didn't matter to me. She was gorgeous. Her picture was on the cover of *Life* magazine that week, biting a rhinestone earring. But she didn't consider herself a success yet because she wasn't appreciated as a good actress. Her work in class was so vulnerable and personal. I marveled at her risk-taking in front of young actors like me, who, as part of the class, would dare to criticize her work. She was so serious about participating, she called my friend Phil Roth to ask him to act in a scene with her.

"Hello, Phil, this is Marilyn," she said. And then, to identify herself to him, "You know, Marilyn from class."

Now, Renée Wexler was asking Marilyn Monroe, the epitome of glamour in a mink coat, babushka, dungarees and a white cotton blouse, "How did you get skin like that?"

"Well," she laughed, "today before I came, I took a hot bath for three hours."

"Uh-huh."

"Then I rubbed Vaseline all over because my skin is dry."

"Uh-huh."

"That's it."

"What do you eat every day?" I asked, hoping to find her secret there.

"I eat grapes. A lot of grapes. I have a sweet tooth and the grapes satisfy my craving."

"Uh-huh. Thanks."

So for the next few weeks, I ate grapes. Red. Green. Black. Frozen. Pits and all. Hoping to look like her. I kept looking in the mirror for her laughing face, but it was only mine looking back. At least it was laughing.

One day when I did a scene, Lee asked me, "What kind of parts do you want to play?"

"Romantic," I said, embarrassed.

"Do you think you look that way?"

"What's the matter with how I look?"

"You look general—" he answered.

That's the worst thing he could have said to me. The next day I came to class with my hair up and a curl at the nape of my neck, but he just stared at me. The next day, I tied on a long hairpiece, still he stared. Two weeks later, he said, "Do you know how you wore your hair yesterday? That was romantic." It was wonderful that he thought I had finally arrived at a romantic look, but I honestly couldn't remember how I had worn my hair the day before.

Meanwhile, I supported myself demonstrating tube dresses in the window of a five-and-ten on Broadway. I pretended to be English to make my job more fun. I drew crowds because I kidded the dress I was selling and people were laughing, but buying it.

"Step right up, ladies. It's the fashion sheath smock everyone's talking about, for $3.98, brought to you by Mavis of England, that's I. Put it on, fold it once, you have your jewel neckline effect; twice, your boating neckline effect; thrice, your Peter Pan collar. Now you add your pins, your clips, your jewels, your pearls. When I was in my hometown, London, England, recently, I demonstrated it for her Royal Highness Princess Margaret Rose, and I said to her, 'What do you think of this smock, Margaret?' And she said to me, 'Mavis, stunning.' When I was in Holland recently, I ran into the Queen Mother Wilhelmina herself, and I said, 'Wilhelmina, how about an endorsement?' And she said to me, 'Mavis, I live in it. Wherever I go, I wear it.' People say, 'There she is, Queen Wilhelmina, wearing her same old-fashioned *shmatte* again, for only $3.98.'"

I was so successful at my five-and-ten pitch that it made me think I should use more theatrical methods to draw attention to myself. As I passed the pet counter in Woolworth's, I had a brainstorm—turtles. I would give out turtles and pet food to people who could hire me. I would paint my name on each turtle and add a photo sticker of myself with my phone number on it. They would feed it each day and think of me and call me for a part. I bought the turtles, painted them and left them outside the offices of 150 agents, producers and advertising agencies who might give me work. And, miracle of miracles, I started to get calls from my turtles.

A man with a thick Italian accent called. "Miss Taylor, I am producing a movie in New York and I saw your picture on a turtle this morning at the talent agency. Come to see me at the Regency Hotel and I'll tell you what I have in mind for you."

"Sure, I'll be right over."

I studied the photo of myself on the turtle sticker. I did look like an Italian movie star. There was something basic in my full, open mouth. No lipstick, but plenty of lip gloss on my mouth, outlined with brown pencil.

"Come in, come in," the Italian producer said. "I was just sitting down to my spaghetti. Would you like some?"

"No, thanks," I said, smiling. I didn't want him to think I was interested in just a free dinner.

"I love your face, Miss Taylor. Since my movie agent showed it to me, it burned a hole right here," and he leaped from the table and grabbed my behind.

"I am a serious actress. I brought you a copy of what the critic from the *Daily News* said about me. If you let go of me, I'll get it from my bag."

"You don't have to show me nothing," he said, holding my behind tighter. "I told you, I love your face."

"Stop that," I said, kicking him in the shins.

"Ah, you know how to make a man's crotch itch with desire," he said, chasing me and unzipping his fly.

I ran to the door.

"Don't touch that door," he said. "Or I break your head open and I cut your throat in a million pieces."

He grabbed me by the hair and spun me around. "Now I do it to you like you never have it done before," he said, lifting me up in his arms and carrying me, puffing, to the bedroom. "Look, I don't want to scream," I said. "But just because you saw my picture on a turtle you got the wrong idea. Let's get to know each other, and then, who knows?"

"No, afterward we going to know plenty," he said, throwing me on the bed and pulling at my pants.

Suddenly, he jumped up and cried, "It's no good! He won't get hard!" He zipped up his pants. "How old are you?"

"Twenty-four," I said, grabbing my pants from the floor.

"Too old," he said. "I can no longer make love when the flower is opened so long. I have a wife. A mistress. But once a woman gets the lines here or under here, I lose my desire. I thought you were younger. Eighteen, nineteen. I eat aphrodisiac in my pasta there, and I am hard as a rock," he said, putting pills in his mouth and swallowing them without water.

"So, I guess a part in your picture is out, huh?" I said, standing at the door.

"Wait," he said. "There is an old whore who dies on the Brooklyn Bridge from bullets. I give you that if you keep your mouth shut that I did nothing."

"Pinky swear," I said.

"Okay," he said. "Eat some spaghetti. I love your face."

Italian Producer's Aphrodisiac Diet

Breakfast: Prunes and calamari
Lunch: Artichoke flowers and spaghetti
Oysters
Lobster diablo
Dinner: Veal alla milanese and spaghetti
Figs and prosciutto

Even though it got me a part, I decided there must be another way. Back at the movie agent's office, I knocked on the door, and when there was no answer, I walked in and pulled my sticker off the turtle in the sandbox and went home. As it turned out, that turtle was the only one that lived. The other 149 died one by one from the stickers keeping the air out of their pores.

I only worked one day on *Lust*. I ran across the bridge in a long shot and I fell to the ground riddled with bullets in a close-up and I died beautifully. For a year, I used *Lust* on my résumé under "Starred in Foreign Films." But when the movie opened and only played on the second half of the bill at drive-in theaters in the Midwest, I realized I could never win an award. People have to see your work to nominate you. It seemed as if my life was at a dead end. All I had to show for my acting career was classes, classes and more classes.

And odd jobs. There wasn't a restaurant or nightclub in New York City that I didn't work at, or get fired from for leaving to go to an acting audition. Riker's, Brass Rail, Toots Shor, Copacabana, Latin Quarter, Metropole—waitress, hat check, cigarette girl, camera girl and finally union organizer. I was fired from Barton's candy store for being "partners" with them. For every piece of candy I sold, I ate one. I put on twenty pounds in a month. When I asked the manager why she was letting me go, she pointed to my huge rear end.

I always was fixated on food. Once there was a fire at the Tip Toe Inn on Broadway. I was eating a piece of chicken on the Chicken and Chicken Fat Diet that was popular in the fifties. The theory was that the high protein burned the fat if that was *all* you ate, but if you got a snip of lettuce in your mouth you *gained*.

Chicken and Chicken Fat Diet

Breakfast: 2 chicken legs
Lunch: 4 chicken wings and 2 spoons chicken fat
Dinner: 1 chicken breast

Someone stuck their head in the kitchen where I was devouring my wings and yelled, "Fire, fire!" Do you know I sat there at the table and finished my lunch before I ran out? I was a literal slave to my food!

And interesting men. There wasn't an exciting actor in New York that I didn't have something to do with, although I never slept with them. I was too afraid to merge sex with the art of acting, so I just talked to them the whole time for fear that sex would interfere with my career.

STEVE MCQUEEN. I met him in Hansen's drugstore. He asked me how he should go about becoming an actor. I told him to study with Lee and have his picture taken by Bruno of Hollywood, as I had done. Three years later, I was playing the small part of a drug addict in *Hatful of Rain* in Philadelphia. Steve pulled up in front of the theater in a red Ferrari. I then asked him how I should go about becoming an actress and how he stayed so thin. He said he skipped a meal every day to have pizza and beer at night.

WARREN BEATTY. I met him in a casting office.

"Excuse me," he said to me. "You came in here with short hair. Then you went in the ladies' room and came out with a long ponytail. Why?"

"These casting people have no imagination. I wanted to give them two different looks."

His favorite diet was Cosmo's Nibbling Crash Diet.

Cosmo's Nibbling Crash Diet

Breakfast: ½ cantaloupe
11 A.M.: 1 hard-boiled egg
Lunch: 3 ounces broiled hamburger, 2 dill pickles
4 P.M.: 1 medium apple
Dinner: ¼ cup tomato juice
6 ounces broiled fish
Green salad
11 P.M.: 1 glass of skim milk

(Lose four pounds in seven days.)

We talked about who was a better actor, Gielgud or Olivier. He invited me up to his apartment to listen to their Shakespearean performances on records. I told him he wasn't old enough for me.

MARLON BRANDO. I picked him up in the Thalia movie house on Ninety-fifth Street near Broadway, at a Japanese movie. I sat down next to him and said, "Are you going to leave me alone?"

"I'm not doing anything."

"I know. Why not?"

He asked me to share a cab downtown to the Village. We talked about Kabuki theater acting. He got out on Fourteenth Street and stuck me with the meter. He gave me his number to call if I knew anyone who wanted to study Kabuki with him. I went eight times to his Kabuki class just to hear him talk. He took me to the Ashram on Seventy-second Street to have authentic Indian food. He said he always wanted it "spicy and sweet."

JOHN WAYNE. I met him in his trailer when he was on location for *The Cowboy and the Lady*. I crawled out from under his bed while he was eating dinner. I told him I admired how he had mastered the first step in acting—talking like himself in his own voice. I was having great difficulty doing that. He asked me why I didn't want to be me when I was pretty enough for all normal purposes. He gave me his recipe for liver, bacon and onions, his favorite dish. I never forgot it.

CARY GRANT. I was an extra for two days in a movie he filmed in New York. I rode the carousel in Central Park all day. He was so handsome I couldn't take my eyes off him. Once he caught me staring at him. He sighed deeply as if to say, "I know you want to be the star of this movie." He started as an extra too. At lunchtime he ate two frankfurters on a roll with mustard and sauerkraut. I was so disillusioned— my mother had told me she read in *Prevention* magazine he lived on dairy products only.

JAMES DEAN. He saw me do a scene in class and said he liked my work. He invited me to see him in a preview of *The*

Immoralist on Broadway to criticize him before the show opened. He was so charismatic in the play I asked *him* to tell *me* what he was doing. He played Louis Jourdan's lover and he never spoke a word. He projected his inner dialogue so strongly he didn't need words. He told me, "Speaking is the least important thing an actor does. Loving and listening is what counts." He drank "Golden Blood," a broth he made from soaking dried apricots.

GEORGE MAHARIS. I acted with him in class, and he was so exciting I shook when he touched me. He cooked me Japanese vegetables in a wok. He was arrested for carrying a real gun to class to use in our scene. The police called Lee Strasberg. When Lee said George was a method actor he was released without being charged.

ROD STEIGER. I did a scene with him at the Actors' Studio. I couldn't hear a word he was saying but it wasn't important. He was so intense. He was on The Boston Police Diet to keep his weight down.

Boston Police Diet

Breakfast: ¼ cup wheat germ before breakfast
Steak and eggs, hamburger and eggs, bacon and eggs or ham and eggs

Lunch: ¼ cup wheat germ
Tuna, salmon, sardines or roast beef
Green salad

Dinner: ¼ cup wheat germ
Meat, fish or poultry
Green salad or cooked green vegetable

(May have ½ grapefruit or unsweetened juice once or twice daily.)

On the weekends I went with my friend Sue Mengers, who later became a superstar's agent, to Fire Island to meet men who were "civilians" (eligibles not in show business).

One Friday night we walked into a coffee shop on Beach Lane, exhausted from walking and "looking." A petite, young blonde was sitting there knitting and looking disgusted. When she saw us eyeing the place, she said, "Go back on the ferry, girls. I've combed the island and there is not one male heterosexual to be had this week-end." That was Joan Rivers.

I was twenty-three and I started singing blues songs in a club on West Fifty-second Street. There were two people on the bill—me and a female impersonator. When I came out, everyone thought I was the female impersonator. A gangster came in every night and requested that I sing "I Gotta Get Hot." One night I heard that two people were shot on the street. The gangster and his bodyguard came running in and told me to sing.

"You want an alibi, is that it?" I said as a joke.

"Shut up and sing," he said, "or you'll have a permanent sore throat."

I sang "his" song about twenty-five times that night.

I moved out of my parents' house and into a hotel in Hell's Kitchen on Tenth Avenue and Forty-second Street. It was very sordid, but it was cheap and centrally located. The first night I slept with the lights on so I could see the fleas that bit me.

Then one day before Lee's class, I auditioned for the *Tonight* show as a singer. I figured I'd sing "Blue Moon" because it had won me the runner-up prize after the accordion player who did "Lady of Spain" fast on the *Original Amateur Hour* when I was eighteen. I started to sing and my zipper broke. Luckily, I had with me my zipper repair kit, which I had demonstrated in Macy's, so I demonstrated it for them. "Fixes all your zippers, and there's no sewing. Just slip it in, snap it on, and pull it up." I started talking about my life, and the turtles, and I said that *TV Guide* was doing a story on me, which wasn't true. Producers Monty Morgan and Bob Shanks said simultaneously, "You're hired."

"As a singer?"

Bob Shanks said, "No, great singers are a dime a dozen, but good talkers are hard to find." Jack Paar was on vacation, and Joey Bishop was subbing. Some big star canceled at the last minute. He asked me to appear that night on Jack's show to *talk*. What a break. I called *TV Guide* and told the editor a very talented girl was to make her debut tonight and be sure to watch.

"Who?" the feature editor asked.

"Me. Renée Taylor. Watch."

Now that everything was in motion, I was paralyzed with nerves. I was given a glass of water in the wings before I went on, and I told Joey Bishop I spilled it on myself from shaking so much. That's why my dress was all wet. Then Joey Bishop asked me to do my demonstration of the dress I sold in the five-and-ten, and I was a big hit with the audience. Then I started telling him about the macrobiotic diet I was on. I had gone to a Japanese health camp run by Dr. Oshawa, who had been arrested for putting some people on this diet and they died. I, however, was still on brown rice and vegetables.

Dr. Oshawa's Rice Diet

Breakfast: Brown rice and vegetables
Lunch: Brown rice and vegetables
Dinner: Brown rice and vegetables

The *Tonight* show received hundreds of inquiries about the diet and one about me.

The inquiry came from Goodman Ace (everyone called him Goody), who was at home watching the show. He wrote the *George Burns and Gracie Allen Show*, and he was currently writing the *Perry Como Show*. The next day he called me. "You remind me of Gracie Allen. I'm going to put you on television and make you a star."

"Who are you?" I asked.

"Your fairy godmother. Where do you live? I'll take you to lunch."

"Forty-second Street and Tenth Avenue. Over the meat market."

"I don't believe you."

"Why not?" I said. "I get great buys on my chicken there."

The next day his limousine was waiting on the street for me. He asked me how much of what I'd said on the air was true.

"All of it and none of it. I'm a comedienne, and whatever I do is a comedy routine done from a funny point of view."

"That's what I thought," he said. "I knew you were gifted. I'm going to put you on Perry's show every week."

I would be doing comedy each week with the biggest names in movies, theater and television. I would be making $750 a week, and Goodman Ace was crazy about me. I wasn't sure if it was as a talent or as a woman, but I was too scared to ask.

A few days later I was back on the *Tonight* show with Jack Paar. I sang a song that I had done on *Talent Sixty* called "Tennessee Williams' Heroine," about a stripper thinking about playing great parts while stripping. At the end of the show Jack said, "You have a job with me once a week for as long as you like."

"You're kidding," I said.

"Why would I kid about a thing like that?"

I was a hit on both shows, Jack's and Perry's.

Then I got a call to appear at the Bon Soir as the comedienne on the bill with a new singer, Barbra Streisand. Barbra and I became good friends, and we were so poor then that we shared a pair of stockings. All my earnings were going to pay back Lee Strasberg and my psychiatrist, Maria Bernstein, who had let me run up bills of about $3,000 each. Barbra and I both had very "physical" acts, and we'd get a run onstage every performance. I'd come offstage and hand my stockings to her to put on.

She was always worried about her weight, but to me her figure was perfect. I would bring tabouli—bulgur, tomatoes, scallions, parsley and mint—to work, and we'd eat it after the show.

"Is this going to make me thin or fat?" Barbra asked.

"Neither. Just healthy and gorgeous."

She was insecure then, and she'd ask me which song to sing first. Years later she'd call me from a phone booth to ask which song to sing first at the White House. I said, "I told you ten years ago what to sing and you didn't listen, and look where it got you. So I'm not telling you anymore!"

When Barbra had just won her Academy Award and sold a million record albums, my mother ran into her mother.

"Mrs. Kind, did you hear Renée has a new apartment on Central Park West, she's reading for a Broadway play with Walter Matthau, she's lost 20 pounds and she's a size eight? So, how's your Barbra doing?" my mother asked.

On the *Como Show* I met all of my idols: Betty Grable, Ginger Rogers, Marlene Dietrich. I was tongue-tied. All I could say the first day was, "So, you're Betty Grable." I followed them around all day, and when I worked up the courage I'd ask them what they ate to look that beautiful, and I'd eat it too.

Betty Grable ate lamb chops and steamed vegetables; Ginger Rogers ate bananas and milk; Marlene Dietrich favored carrot juice, wheat germ and honey.

"How can I get legs like yours?" I asked Marlene.

"Have a grandmother who has beautiful legs."

I heard this story about Dietrich on the *Como Show*. When the cameraman, who was an old friend, played back her scene on the monitor, she complained to him, "Why don't I look as beautiful as the way you made me look the last time we worked together?" "Forgive me, Marlene, but I'm twenty years older now," he answered.

One night when Jerry Lewis was a guest on the *Tonight* show, he told me, "If you're ever in California, look me up." So I flew to California the next day and said, "Okay, I'm here."

"There's no part for you in the picture I'm doing now."
"Who wrote it?" I asked.
"I did."
"Okay," I said. "Just tear out five pages of the script and write in five new pages with a part for me."
"You've got guts," Jerry answered. That's how I got my first movie part, in *The Errand Boy*.

When I saw myself on the screen, I couldn't believe it. I was so disappointed. I had this fantasy of how I would look. I don't know what I was expecting—Garbo in *Camille*, I guess. I looked too heavy, and not very feminine. My weight made me look like an eleven-year-old tomboy.

After working with Jerry Lewis and doing the fifth *Perry Como Show*, I did a switch on Pygmalion and taught Bing Crosby to speak with a New York accent and tense up. I had my own fan club, started by people who wrote in. That's when I started seeing my Philadelphia society boyfriend again. I recommended him to Goodman Ace because they were doing a takeoff of *Hamlet* and I thought he'd be good at it. They hired him and then fired him for showing up drunk. I took him home to my apartment to sober him up, and he never left. At twenty he had appeared off-Broadway as Hamlet right after leaving the academy, and doing a jokey *Hamlet* sketch now made him feel a failure. I identified with him, even though I was starting to do well, because it was more painful for me to feel like a success. Wasn't there a price for success? Who would I owe it to? Like the princess in "Rumpelstiltskin," I always thought someone would come to claim it.

I worried that I wasn't good enough to be making so much money on two shows and have a movie career too. I thought that sitting at the feet of these great acting teachers I would absorb a lot of knowledge by osmosis. Sometimes I would fall asleep—it was such a warm, safe place to be. Once I woke up in Lee's class and at first I thought I was dreaming. Marilyn Monroe was onstage doing a sense memory of the wind. She gave herself totally to the experience. After class, I walked down the street with her.

"I tried the grape diet. It didn't do anything for me," I said.

"Really? Try hot water and lemon for one day and then do hot water with orange juice for two. I'm on the third day."

"I never knew who I wanted to be until now—you. I'm finally making $750 a week, and I have this awful fear of giving up control. But I saw from your exercise, you have to lose control to find yourself. You are the wind, Marilyn. That's why I want to be you."

"When you become me, Renée, tell me what it's like. I always wanted to be Irene Dunne."

At that moment, having Marilyn Monroe as a friend in class, Goody as my fairy godmother looking after my television career, a handsome, decadent actor at home—in a flea-bitten bed because I was too busy to look for a new apartment—I was actually envious of myself for the first time. I gave a party at my apartment a week later, after the taping of the show that "Philadelphia Society" was fired from. When I sent out invitations, I was happy that I had played Ophelia to Jimmy Durante's Polonius. "Philadelphia Society" had invited his family to come to the taping of the show earlier in the week. I invited my parents too, and my friend Marilyn from class, never dreaming she would come. She wore her dark glasses, mink coat and babushka, and everyone knew it was her in the audience, and the air was filled with excitement. And then the nightmare began. "Philadelphia Society" came to the taping and booed. Someone in the back of the house yelled, "Sit down, you moron." It was my father. Boy, was he upset. The scene was going great guns, getting belly laughs until "Philadelphia Society" interrupted.

Goodman Ace was pacing in the back of the house. He yelled, "Stop tape, get that man out of here. He's ruining the show."

They carried Philly out of the theater reciting, "Oh, what a noble mind is here o'er thrown."

I thought, He's trying to get me fired too. I wasn't angry, I was touched. He was so pathetic. And I was guilty about my success, so I needed distractions to get my mind off how well I was doing; and then each day I gave a small piece of myself away until it was all gone. Also, it was great to have someone crazier than me in my life to make me look good!

All of those concerns became trifles, because that night I lost my father to his first and last heart attack. After the show he was the first one back to my dressing room.

"What a mess the show was, Daddy! Did you like me anyway?" I asked him.

"Why don't you come in business with me part-time? So you have something to fall back on," he said. He was selling men's dry goods.

"I will if you come into show business with me part-time. We'll both have something to fall back on," I answered, trying to have a deep communication with him. Somehow I felt we were just missing getting in touch with each other.

The party, like the show, was surreal. Marilyn Monroe sat on the bed in my hotel room explaining Stanislavski to Jimmy Durante. Philly's mother showed my mother and father pictures of Philly as a baby, dressed like a little girl in velvet and lace from a charmed-children contest twenty years ago. They were stunned by her lack of good taste in showing her son's baby picture on the night when he practically ruined my big show. The *Hamlet* scene had to be cut. Goody sulked in a corner, furious with me.

"You'd better promise me you won't have anything to do with that man again, because he'll do this every time," he said.

Just then the door opened and Philly appeared with his father holding his arm. Philly wore a porkpie hat and a long winter coat down to his ankles. He took it off and he was stark naked underneath. Everyone gasped. My father slid off the couch onto the floor, and an ambulance was called. He had had a heart attack. I rode with him in the ambulance to the hospital. Goody took my mother in a taxi. She was afraid she'd have a heart attack too.

"Daddy," I said. "I love you. I never cared about anything but you. Everything I try to be is for you to love me. Tell me you love me too."

"Don't put pressure on a dying man," the ambulance driver said.

"Daddy," I said. "You can't die. Nobody's father dies at forty."

"The first attack usually kills," the ambulance driver said.

"Be quiet," I said to the driver. "Tell me you love me, Daddy, just once. You can't die without saying you love me."

My father lifted himself up on one arm as if he was going to say something, but then he just stared at me as though he'd forgotten what he was going to say. Then he lay down and I knew he was gone.

"Daddy," I sobbed hysterically. "What were you going to say?"

Was he going to say he loved me, or not? He was so needy he couldn't reach out to anyone. Whenever the phone rings, I think maybe that's him calling to tell me from beyond. "I thought it over and I do love you and I'm glad I had you as a daughter because I could tell how much you wanted me to be happy."

Six months later I keeled over on the street with a burst appendix, and I began to have recurring dreams that I was on trial for my father's death. I always woke up before the jury came in. What if they brought in a verdict of guilty? But back then, the day after my father died, Philly wanted the blame all to himself. He showed up at my mother's house wearing a sheet wrapped around him. My mother called me just as I was leaving for the new show, first day of rehearsal.

"Renée," she said. "Come quick. I have no experience with mental illness that's abnormal. He insists he's Moses and that he killed Daddy. And he told me this in Yiddish."

There was a bottle of Thorazine with a doctor's name on it

on Philly's night table. I called the number.

"Hello, Doctor. He's hallucinating. What should I do?" I asked.

"See that he takes his Thorazine four times a day, and get him to come back to the institute as soon as possible," he said.

"Institute?" I said.

"He's been in and out his whole life."

"Oh, God. Is there anyone Jewish in his family?" I asked. "He's speaking Yiddish."

"Oh, no. It's self-taught. He's been many people from the Old Testament over the years. It's his compensation for his family's anti-Semitism. That's the nature of his schizophrenia."

"You mean he's schizophrenic, Doctor?" I was suddenly terrified.

"That's correct. But the seeds are in all of us. A little shock therapy and he'll be fine."

I figured that if my love could cure Philly, then maybe my father in heaven could forgive me for his dying and my living and being a hit on *Perry Como* and the *Tonight* show.

As I walked down the street to my mother's house, I heard a blood-curdling scream coming from the bedroom. It was Philly, not my mother.

"I broke my own commandment," he was yelling in Yiddish, waving a butcher's knife toward himself. "Now slaughter me, as I slaughtered him."

"Meshugenah," my mother said. *"Meshugenah."*

"Look," I said, "you're upsetting my mother. My idol, Judy Holliday, is going to be at rehearsal, and I've got to meet her. I'll drop you off at the institute on the way downtown. And fear not. The seeds of schizophrenia are in all of us."

I said it so matter-of-factly that Philly went along willingly to the institute. I was envious of him going to such a friendly, cheery place while my career with its upward climb was getting scarier and scarier.

I was so guilty about my father and Philly's breakdown that

food was always talking to me. George White was a friend of Goody's, and he arranged for me to audition for a starring role in a revival of *George White's Scandals*. The night before my audition I woke up in the middle of the night, and I must have sleepwalked over to the refrigerator, because I don't know how I got there.

I heard a voice inside my head say, "Sweetheart, we both know tonight's the night. So when rape is inevitable, relax and enjoy it. The kindest thing I can do for you when you have an important opportunity is to fatten you up for the kill of success. You won't be able to eat for a long time if you're hired. So, let's have an evening to remember. You've got the rest of your life to be thin, but this is the last time you can lose control with a farewell to salami. A salute to spaghetti marinara cold! Now finish off the chocolate ripple ice cream in the freezer like a good girl. The wild time you have tonight will insulate you against the terror that's waiting for you with stardom. I bet your feet and your nose are cold. Load up to warm up. Some hot chocolate and a marshmallow. Kim Novak has it—why not you? You've been such a brave girl to even think of cutting down on food. You deserve to have an Oreo for courage. It's not your fault that you're fat. It's your mother's. It's show business. It's men. You eat a bird's portion of bacon and you gain 2 pounds. Have a leg of lamb. One won't hurt you. Tomorrow you won't eat anything. When can you do this again? How many calories are there in two loaves of bread? Two thousand. You'll walk it off. Tomorrow you'll walk to Brooklyn. You feel bad anyway because you're so fat, why not have a good time to show for it? Gain a pound tonight. Tomorrow you'll take off three. Tomorrow morning you'll be forced to diet. Better yet, wait until after the holidays. Thanksgiving is only four days away and thirty-four to Christmas. It's silly to start now and then gorge yourself with goodies at Christmastime and then begin all over again. Wait for the summertime and I'll help you. Open your mouth. Here come three ears of corn. You're a bottomless well when you're eating to forget yourself. Here comes the custard filling with maraschino cherries. And then we'll have a whole liverwurst. Wash it down with a jar of hot peppers. Maybe George White will feel sorry for you and hire you because of how hard you worked staying up all night studying food poisoning. It's the kind of eating course you keep taking and you never graduate from."

The next day I was as stoned as if I had had hard drugs. I just sat on the piano and sang, "I Gotta Get Hot," because I couldn't move. George White thought I was very seductive. "A new Helen Morgan," he said.

I decided not to tell him that I was kidding in the number that he thought was for real. If he thought that was sexy, then I would be sexy.

On opening night Orson Welles, S. J. Perelman and Alfred Hitchcock were in the audience. Orson asked me to join him at his table after the show. He was very flattering to me, and he seemed very lonely. I couldn't believe what he ate—three hens and six different kinds of French fruit tarts. It looked like someone's last meal. I heard that the night he died he had dined on a very similar feast at Ma Maison.

"How was it being married to Rita Hayworth?" I asked him.

"She was very beautiful, but I caught her stealing my chocolate ice cream out of the freezer."

I was so nervous about being introduced to Alfred Hitchcock that I said, "Pleased to meet you, Mr. Hotchpick."

"Hotch*potch!*" he corrected.

S. J. Perelman was too shy to meet me. He sent me flowers instead. The next day he called to take me to lunch. He thought I was very funny. He "got" what I was doing with the supposedly sexy song George White had me do in the show. He said he wanted to write a part for me in his new play, *The Beauty Part*. Eventually, it was cut out.

I didn't feel worthy of the attention from all these wonderful men—Perelman, Welles, White, Ace. One by one, I hurt them with my inability to receive what they could teach me as I've learned to do now. One night George White wanted to try a new number in the show. The tenor was to sing "You Are Love" to me as he swung me on a swing, wearing a picture hat and a *Gone with the Wind* gown. As a joke, at the end of the song, I smiled at him. I had blacked out my teeth. George White took it so personally he came backstage practically in tears.

"Renée, you are making fun of me. You think I'm a sentimental old fool."

"George, I'm sorry. I didn't want people to notice I've gotten so fat that I was coming out of my costume. So I blacked my teeth as a distraction."

He fired me on the spot.

Then, when they heard I was fired, S. J. Perelman and Goodman Ace wanted to help me work on a comedy act.

"I'd rather do it myself," I said. I never knew how to ask for help when I needed it and when to do it myself because I didn't need it. That's part of the compulsive eater's disease. Only when I stopped eating and committed myself to abstinence between meals did I begin to discover my real problems.

I began working at a supper club on the East Side. I wrote the act myself, onstage—making it up as I went along as I had seen Lenny Bruce do. It was daring, but the customers seemed to like it. Lenny watched me one night and afterward asked me for a date. I was surprised at how shy he was. "I heard you're a real ladies' man," I said.

"Really? I was sure you'd make a pass at me."

I went out with Lenny several times, and I wrote a scene about him. The man keeps telling the woman how low he is, and she is very understanding no matter what he says. Finally he says, "I'm the lint on the earthworm's navel," and she answers, "Ech!"

Lenny asked me to be a character witness at his profanity trial. I said I would, but he overdosed on heroin before I was called.

One night, a Welsh actor who was on Broadway in the play *Luther* came in, and during one of my songs he kept yelling out, "Bloody marvelous." After my set, he told me I had won his heart and we were going to get married in three months. "Great," I said. "What's your name so I don't forget it?"

For the next few months, we made the rounds of all the saloons nightly after mine closed. He drank Irish whiskey and recited bawdy poetry to me. Because I wanted to look ladylike and elegant, at his suggestion I went on a diet that was the rage of England: the Queen Mother's Royal Diet. Evidently, Princess Di still uses it, because when Prince Charles was asked if Princess Di was anorexic, he said, "No. She just uses the Royal Diet." For the duration of my whole hot and heavy romance with the Welshman I ate like the queen.

The Queen Mother's Royal Diet

Breakfast: Oranges, kippers, eggs and toast
Lunch: Apples, salmon mousse
Dinner: Pears and fish pâté
Kidney pie

(The premise being: For breakfast, eat like a king; for lunch, like a prince; for dinner, like a pauper.)

I got fatter and fatter.

I auditioned for a show directed by Elaine May, *The Third Ear.* She had seen me in a play with Tom Poston and came backstage and asked me to try out for a new improvisational revue. I had never written for this kind of show before, but now, with her encouragement (and she is the best), I was writing on my feet. My friend Louise Lasser was in the show, and her boyfriend Woody Allen came every night to watch Louise, Peter Boyle, Reni Santoni and me perform.

I got a contract for a year. After six months I asked Elaine to let me out of my contract so I could go to England to marry the Welshman. Elaine said, "If he loves you he'll wait for you six months."

He didn't. At first, he wrote that he couldn't live without

me—please come right away. Then, after three months, I called him, and when a woman answered the phone, I knew. My body went through an actual physical withdrawal from missing him. That's when I started vegetable-juice fasting, ballet class and dating loads of men.

For the first time there was safety in numbers. And they weren't all actors. A well-known psychiatrist called me a love huntress, and I was. There was a documentary film director who had been married five times, and I considered for a moment being number six. His last wife set fire to his films. After he insulted her, she got so angry at him she lit matches and blew them out. One night after several of his put-downs I caught myself lighting matches and blowing them out.

A B-movie producer who owned a film studio in the Village and who was married kept proposing to me. He said he'd get a divorce if I would move in with him. I met him while I was working as an actress on the *Guy Lombardo* dance series on television. They needed an actor and an actress to pretend to be great dancers, à la Fred and Ginger, who came every week to dance to Guy Lombardo's music because they loved it. For thirteen weeks, I danced to that music and it was hell. I remember saying to Guy Lombardo when he started playing "Cherry Pink and Apple Blossom White," "Didn't you just play that?" It all sounded alike.

The producer told me they were having readings upstairs for three B movies—*The Mugger, Street of Sinners* and *Cop Hater*. I was in such a silly state going from one room to another that I got all three jobs. I followed my small parts in these three movies with an even bigger streetwalker part in *Four Boys and a Gun*.

4
A LITTLE OLDER FAT

I was on an upswing in my career, and for the first time my weight was down, on the Miracle Protein Reducing Diet, when I met Joe Bologna.

Miracle Protein Reducing Diet

In a glass of fruit or vegetable juice, dissolve 1 tablespoon of unflavored gelatin. Dissolve 1 meat bouillon cube and then mix together. Drink an hour before each meal.

It was 1965, and I felt it was time to get married, because I had been fooling myself into believing that I would get married when I reached a certain point in my career. Then I would make some headway, only to have it all fall apart. For instance, while I was doing those B movies, I was hired to replace someone playing Appassionata Von Climax in *Lil Abner*.

I played the part for two weeks, then Lee Strasberg recommended me for Natasha in *Three Sisters* off-Broadway. I found someone else to replace me in *Lil Abner* so they would let me out of my contract, then *Three Sisters* closed before it opened and I was out of a job. The theater would always be like that.

My friend Bill Hickey told me, "Your career isn't just one thing in your life—it *is* your life."

"But I don't have a life," I said. That's how I knew it was *time*. Practically the next minute after I had that thought, I was introduced to Joe. We both had the same manager, Buddy Allen.

"I want you to meet someone—I think you'll have a comedy rapport with him," Buddy said.

As Joe extended his hand, I looked into his brown eyes. He seemed very open.

"This is Him," I remember thinking. A resting place. And then he laughed at a story I told him about my mother taking me to a meeting of her reincarnation club when I was younger. She introduced each person to me as the former Countess, the former Baron.

"How come everyone here was royalty in their last life? Why are there no garbage collectors, for instance?" I asked.

"Well," my mother said. "I guess they know they wouldn't fit in here."

At the meeting they held a séance to contact the other world. An Indian medium told my mother to tell Sam Brockman "Hello."

"Do you know Sam Brockman?" I asked my mother.

"No."

"Then what's the point?"

"If I ever meet him, I have regards from a dead Indian."

Joe laughed in the places where no one else laughed, because he understood her. I knew he was *it*.

When Buddy Allen introduced us in his office, Joe was with Rudy Deluca, his writing partner. Joe was working at an advertising agency during the day and writing comedy material with Rudy at night. Rudy thought I might like a piece of their material for a one-woman show I was putting together, so they came to my house to show it to me. I read it over and said it was too "jokey." I wanted routines that came directly out of the characters and the situations.

"That will cost you more," Rudy said.

I was about to leave for my first appearance on the *Merv Griffin Show*, so as they went out Joe said jokingly, "Which of us do you want to come back later?"

"You," I said, meaning it, and he gave me his phone number.

I did a comedy monologue from *The Third Ear*, for which the *New York Times* singled me out with a banner headline, "Miss Taylor Excels in a Cast of Five." The next day Merv's producer, Bob Shanks, who had been on the staff at the *Tonight Show*, called and invited me to be on Merv's show. I did so well Merv invited me right back on the air.

"How would you like to be a regular and come on every week and do monologues and sketches with me?" he asked.

"I'm such a fan of yours I'd even be happy to be an irregular."

I was a big hit that first night, and my being an irregular got me talked about. A few people wrote letters asking if they could start a fan club. They said they didn't have much money, but they'd like to wear Renée Taylor Fan Club sweat shirts. I was thrilled. I went down to a wholesale house and got sweat shirts that were irregular and had Elizabeth Taylor's name on them. My fan club put a thin line through Elizabeth and wrote Renée on top of it. We all thought it was funny, and it only cost them half price. We were all on our way to Merv Griffin's Little Theater in New York, wearing the sweat shirts, when we ran into Elizabeth Taylor herself going into Sardi's. She stared at me and the shirt. I started explaining. "See, my name is Renée Taylor—although Taylor isn't my real name. I know it's yours. I think you're wonderful, but these shirts are irregular . . ." I kept making it worse.

Someone in her entourage said, "It's not too dignified."

"How would it be if I made Elizabeth's name larger and mine smaller?" I called after them, but they were already inside the restaurant. Twelve years later a caricature of me was put up on the wall of Sardi's right next to hers. I wrote on it, "I'm so honored to have my face and my name placed, not above or below Elizabeth Taylor, but beside her."

When I got home from Merv Griffin's show that night, around 11:00 P.M. on the day I met Joe, I called him. "You want to come over?" I asked.

"For what?"

"Conversation."

"Okay, but I can't stay long."

Months after that he told me he put down the phone and called Rudy.

"She wants me to come over."

"For what?"

"She says conversation, but I think she wants sex," Joe said.

"Don't go," Rudy said. "You've got too much sex already."

Joe had been seeing a lot of women, but when they got serious, he ran. He had just broken up with a girl and didn't want to get half-involved again.

When I opened my door for him, he looked disappointed. "I thought you'd be in a negligee, holding a whip."

"I considered that outfit, but I didn't want to scare you. So I decided to change my blouse instead," I said.

I imagine that threw him, because he started telling me stories of his many sexual adventures with women since college.

"Why are you telling me this?" I asked. "You don't have to prove anything. I like you. We're not going to have sex, we're going to be intimate."

He was nervous because he knew I was serious. I knew he was perfect for me. Just as I wanted to be a movie star, he wanted to be the Lone Ranger—to perform great deeds without anyone knowing who he was. He seemed honest and sensitive, and he believed in fidelity. He had been an altar boy, and he'd even considered being a priest when he got older. I felt that he would be day-in-day-out happiness. I decided I should try it and see what it was like.

Happiness! All my life I had distracted myself from happiness with my weight problem and with crazy men. I decided to fall in love with Joe Bologna by pretending he was a heel.

When he arrived he said he could only stay a few hours, so I set the alarm for 2:30 A.M. It rang and we were both relieved. I had told him this was going to be a short and sweet whirlwind affair culminating in something permanent, but he didn't believe me.

"You will," I said. "I don't want to talk you into it now though. It's too much work. I just did a show."

A few days later I got a call from Joe's advertising agency to audition for a cereal commercial. At the agency I saw him relate to everyone he worked with in the same way—from the coffee lady to the president of the company—all as equals. I loved that. His staff kept asking me to eat the cereal with more abandon. Finally, I just threw the little round hoops up in the air.

"I'll call you," Joe said.

"I hope you're not one of these guys that say they're going to call and then don't."

I went home and dialed his number. "I thought you said you were going to call. You've had over an hour. How about dinner at my house?"

"I can't. I'm on a special diet. Whipped cream and martinis. The best part is I have to eat everything in order to lose."

Joe Bologna's Whipped Cream and Martini Diet

Breakfast: Orange juice
2 fried eggs
4 slices of bacon
Black coffee
Coffee Break: Favorite cheese
Coffee with whipped cream
Lunch: Martini
Cream of mushroom soup
Chicken salad with mayonnaise
Melon
Coffee with whipped cream

Dinner: Martini (1 or 2)
Shrimp cocktail
Porterhouse steak
Sautéed mushrooms
Asparagus with hollandaise sauce
Tossed salad with Roquefort dressing
Strawberries
Coffee with whipped cream
Evening Snack: Cold chicken
Dry champagne

"Come over. I've got something better," I said.

That night he came over and brought me a gift, a box of cannoli. I lit the candles, brought out the red wine and served him the dinner I had made.

"What is this?" he said, tasting my spaghetti.

"I'm on the Rockefeller Spaghetti Diet," I said.

Rockefeller Spaghetti Diet

Breakfast: Baked peaches in maple syrup
Radish sandwiches
Lunch: Spaghetti with butter and Parmesan cheese
Scallops
Red wine
Dinner: Spaghetti al pesto
Red wine

"It's spaghetti al pesto," I said. "By Buitoni."

"You serve an Italian spaghetti from a can?" he said.

"I eat it all the time. I thought it was the best."

"You teach me conversation—I'm going to teach you pasta," he said, dumping the spaghetti in the trash can.

Sitting over pasta al'amatriciana and Chianti with him a short time later, I knew I had a real sensualist on my hands. He said, "Ooh, I could make love to this spaghetti" (only "make love" wasn't the phrase he used). I wanted to drown myself in his joy and happiness, so I said, "Let's get married."

He said, "I don't even know you."

"But when you do you're going to love me, and then let's get married. It's not just for me, it's for you too. You're thirty. You make $250 a week. You know a lot of girls. Practice loving with me. You can change your mind at any time. It's okay with me. I don't want you if you don't want me."

"Let me get back to you," he said. Then he proceeded to tell me every detail of his life from the moment he was born.

As dawn came up, he was still talking. I walked him home to the West Village to change his clothes before he went to work. A cute girl around twenty was sitting on the stoop waiting for him. She seemed drunk.

"Joey," she cried, slurring her words. "Where have you been all night?"

"Camille, I told you to forget about me," Joey said.

"What's the matter, Joey? Didn't you like the way I boodled?" she asked. "You used to love to boodle me while I sang."

She started singing "Mala Femmina" to him, then asked, "Who's she?" pointing to me.

"Look, Camille, you're drunk now. Let's talk when you're sober," he said, walking her down the stairs. "I'll put you in a cab."

"Oh, no, we'll talk about it in front of your new fat bitch," Camille said, suddenly lunging for my neck. "Witch, bitch," she said, choking me. Joe tried to pull Camille's hands off my throat, but Camille shoved her knee in his groin and Joe landed on the sidewalk.

Suddenly, I squeezed her right breast gently and said, "Beep-beep," as though I were honking a horn. "Beep-beep," I said again, as I gently squeezed her left breast.

Camille stepped back, shocked. "What are you, a dyke? She's a dyke," she yelled to a passerby down the street.

Joe grabbed my arm and we ran up the stairs. He opened the front door quickly and then slammed it shut. We heard her banging on the door as we continued up the inside steps.

"Your beep-beeps saved my life," he said admiringly.

"Who was that?" I asked inside his apartment.

"My ex-secretary. I should never have slept with her."

"We'd better go see this marriage therapist I heard about. I'll make the appointment."

"I don't know. I think we're rushing," Joe said.

"Look, she's seventy-seven and she doesn't have much time left to help. Let's grab her."

Joe handed me the phone.

"Marry him," Maria Bernstein, the therapist I had been seeing off and on for seven years, said to me privately, after spending twenty minutes alone with him. "There's an 80 percent chance he'll make a good husband. He's not that neurotic next to what I've seen lately. And he's so nurturing. You'll be the star in the family."

A few weeks later his mother called me. "Miss Taylor, I understand you vamped my son into an engagement," she said to me.

"Vamped? I wish it was that easy. Your son is not committed to anything but practicing."

"Practicing what?" his mother asked.

"Loving a woman intimately."

"Well, look, Miss. I believe in true love but you only know each other a few weeks. Why don't you not see each other for a year and then if you still want to get engaged, I'll know it's a love that's true."

Joe was listening on the phone and said, "Hey, Ma, why don't I not see you for a year and then I'll know if I feel a true love for you," and he hung up.

A few weeks later I called her to apologize for Joe's hanging up.

"That wasn't my idea," I said. "I respect your feelings. I'd like to get to know you and what you eat."

"Huh?"

"I have a theory it's easier to get to know people if you find out what they eat."

"Sure," she said. "You mean, if I ever come to visit you'll know what to serve."

"Uh-huh." I didn't tell her the whole truth, how I believe that the amount of sugar, flour, caffeine and fat in our diets influences how crazy we behave. Her diet let me know what I was in for.

Josie Bologna's Diet

Breakfast: Pound cake
Coffee with skim milk, 2 sugars
Lunch: Minestrone
Hard roll and butter
Dinner: Spaghetti with clam sauce
Tomato sauce with sugar
Fried potatoes
Fried zucchini
Espresso with 2 sugars

A few minutes later, Joe's father called. He wanted to meet Joe at his apartment to have a talk.

"How can they be against me?" I asked. "They haven't even met me."

"They've seen you on the *Merv Griffin Show*."

I don't know why, but I wasn't really scared of losing him.

I'd had a recurring dream of falling off a cliff into a sea of monsters. Just as I'm about to be eaten, a man's hand reaches to save me. As he pulls me up to the top of the cliff, the dream ends with me saying, "Do me a favor. Let me fall once more and let's see if you can save me again."

I don't know how it would have worked with another man, but with Joey my love of danger served me well. I walked over to his apartment a few hours later. I had a hunch I should take on his father, because I sensed that his resistance to me

would be more than Joe's and his mother's combined.
I was right. The door was wide open. Joe's father sat at the kitchen table with his head in his hands. The television set had been kicked in, and Joe stood in front of a broken window, his hand bleeding.

"What happened?" I asked.

"Tell her what you told me," Joe said to his father.

Mr. Bologna looked at me wearily.

"Okay, I'll tell you. I'm no phony. I say nothing to your back I don't say to your face. I've seen you on television and you look to be a comedian."

"I do?" I looked in the mirror. "I'm certainly not aware of it. I mean, I am a comedienne, but I wouldn't ever want to *look* that way. I always want to look more . . . romantic than that."

"Well, you don't to me and you never will. No matter what you do to yourself, everyone knows you're Jewish and that's something you can't ever change. Once a Jew, always a Jew," he said.

"That's true. That is absolutely true. I'm sorry."

"What kind of an answer is that? Sorry. I'm an old man. You want to give me a heart attack? I have two daughters. I don't care what their husbands look like. But I have only one son, and I'm not going to let him pull something like you on me."

"I understand."

"And if he marries you, even if the Pope himself gives you his blessing, I don't."

"I love you, Mr. Bologna, and I'm touched by your honesty," I said.

"She's a nut," his father told Joe. "A crazy nut."

"Be quiet," Joe said to his father. "You're so stupid. I have a million better reasons for not marrying Renée, and your reason is so small. It's like a fly buzzing around my ear."

"If you have a million better reasons to not get married to her, why are you going to?" his father asked.

"I didn't say it's definite, but I may decide to. I haven't gotten married because I'm scared of getting hurt," Joe said.

"That's why I'm almost thirty and I never came close."

"If he marries you, Miss, I will never recognize you or your kids."

"That's fair," I said. "Could I ask you a personal question?"

"Sure. I'll tell you anything to your face."

"What are you eating? A sample menu? Your food may be making you a trifle oversensitive to me," I said.

"Oh, yeah! Here's what I'm having today."

Tony Bologna's Diet

Breakfast: Macaroni soup
Italian salami and eggs
Lunch: Hot pepper sausage and onions on Italian bread
Dinner: Parmesan cheese and spinach ravioli
Stuffed veal chops
Sautéed potatoes, squash and zucchini
Ricotta cheesecake

"Just what I thought," I said. "If you cut down your salt, fried foods and hard processed meats, you might get to like me. If not, I love you and I forgive you anyway."

"What a nut," he said, shaking his head and going out the door.

The moment I met Joe's father I knew that I would write about him someday, the way I would have to write about my mother. I "knew" what he would say and do in any situation. I was so inspired by his outrageousness, I couldn't wait to share my appreciation of him with the world.

Oddly enough, I was sticking to the Rockefeller Diet even though the pressure around me was mounting—Joe's ambivalence, his parents, my career. Mike Nichols saw me in Elaine May's show and asked me to audition as Anne Jackson's standby in *Luv*. I was a size ten, but my dress was tight when I read for him. I remember thinking, He may not offer me this job—why don't I just "take" it by dazzling him? It worked. When Anne Jackson broke her arm, I got to play for two weeks with Gene Wilder, who was standby for Eli Wallach and Alan Arkin. George Abbott was in the audience, and he wrote me this letter:

"Dear Renée, I can't imagine anyone better than you. Please come see me."

I was ecstatic. Everything was perfect. Except that I'm a compulsive eater always in danger of bingeing, and I was saving up for a big one to strike at the least opportune moment. Joe and I had dinner with his parish priest.

"How can I promise to be faithful for the rest of my life, Father?" Joe asked.

"The very fact that you asked that question means you will be—as long as you live your life in the question," the priest said. I think that is great advice, although then Joe and I both looked at each other quizzically, not sure what it meant.

"Let's have an engagement party," I suggested.

Joe said, "Okay, but don't invite any of my friends and family. I'll give you a ring too, if you don't show it to anyone."

"Great."

Elaine May said, "I'll give the engagement party. I'll order food for a hundred people. If no one comes, that's okay. We'll freeze the food. Right, David?" Her husband, David Rubenfine, agreed. The three of us knew that at the last minute Joe would invite his friends and family, but we thought it would be a fun party even if he didn't.

"Renée and Joe seem like the perfect couple, Mrs. Taylor," Elaine's mother said to my mother.

"My name is Wexler, not Taylor. Frieda Wexler, and I'm a star in my own right," I heard my mother reply.

My mother was noncommittal about Joe, but only because she had had such a harrowing experience with Philly. About my career, she was both excited and confused, not understanding why it wasn't as satisfying as she'd hoped it would be to live vicariously through me.

One night shortly before our engagement party, Joe and I were sitting at the bar in the Elegante Night Club in Brooklyn where I was playing, and he started crying.

"I've never told any woman this, but I really love . . . my father. You remind me of him."

In the sixties, everyone was into hating their parents. It was so refreshing that he felt that way. I took it as a great compliment, and I fell deeply in love with him, ambivalence and all.

One morning soon after, I was coming out of a vegetable juice place on Madison Avenue called I Love Juicy when I heard a car horn and a woman's voice calling my name. I turned to see who it was.

"Renée, it's me—Marilyn." It was. Marilyn Monroe.

"Hi," I said, crossing the street. "How are you feeling?"

I noticed her eyes were red and her hair was disheveled. She wore an old bathrobe and sweater, and her dungarees were frayed around the bottom.

"I'm here to find out," she said. "I have an appointment with the iridologist, and I'm just killing time."

"What's an iridologist?"

"He can look into your eyes and tell you what foods your body is craving and the missing vitamins that will correct your mineral imbalance," Marilyn said.

"It sounds wonderful. Guess what? I met the one I've been waiting for. Best of all, he believes in fidelity."

"Oh, sure," Marilyn laughed.

"Really. He was going to be a priest when he was young. He's sexy, but he has tremendous integrity."

"Gee, will you let me know if your friend has a nice friend for me?"

"I sure will."

That night I said to Joe, "Do you know anyone who's faithful, loyal and true?"

"For who?" Joe asked.

"Marilyn Monroe. She asked me today. I swear. What about your friend George, or Sal or Rudy? Do you think she'd like any of them?"

We sat up all night talking about who we knew who might be good for Marilyn Monroe. We decided we couldn't swear that any of his friends would be faithful.

Two months later, my friend Marilyn from class was dead from an overdose. When I saw a picture of her on the front page of the *Daily News*, I thought, If only I could have found somebody "nice" for her.

It was time to go pricing catering halls for the wedding. I wanted Tavern on the Green, but it was very expensive—twelve dollars a person.

"Here's all your father's insurance money to pay for the wedding," my mother said.

That night on Merv's show I asked him if he thought it was worth my father's insurance money to have the chicken served at my wedding.

Merv said, "Let me give you the wedding reception and we'll tape it and show it on the show."

Sitting next to Joe in the audience, my mother cried at Merv's generosity. Out on the street, Joe said to me, "Are you crazy? Agreeing to film the reception on Merv's show when I might not even show up? Why would you do that to yourself?"

"Joe, I don't want to pressure you, but I have my gown. I have my figure almost perfect. I have to have the wedding before I lose it all. If you don't come, it's up to you. I'll prepare a speech to cover my embarrassment if you decide to back out. Until then, I am thrilled to have a good friend like Merv Griffin."

Two nights before the wedding, Joe's friends gave him a stag party. Two girls came and stripped. When I found out about it, I called him.

"You are not the man of my dreams—you didn't just pay those women off and send them home," I said. He hung up on me.

Joe's father met him the next morning for breakfast. "Look, there's still time to get out of it. Take the honeymoon tickets and get out of town today. I'll cover for you," Mr. Bologna said.

"Thanks a lot. I was hoping you were going to talk me out of doing just that."

The night before the wedding, either I was scared that Joe

wouldn't show up or that he would, because I had some buttered popcorn, a bag of potato chips, a Mars bar and a diet RC Cola, starting a binge that would last for twenty years. I only came off it briefly to diet for shows I was in, and then I would go right back on the binge, until last year when I formulated my Taylor-Made Diet for life.

I awoke to the smell of chocolate even though there was none in the house. That's what I wanted for breakfast. I guess I was trying to distract myself from the big day by obsessing on which bar of chocolate I was going to have after the ceremony. It seems impossible that I could eat so much that only twelve hours later I couldn't get into my wedding gown, but it's true. I had to let all the seams out.

I was the first one at the church. We didn't know if Joe's father would even show up there, because I was Jewish. His mother said that unless we got married in the church she wouldn't come either. My mother said, "The important thing is mental health." So she didn't care. I had to memorize the speech I would make to the television cameras if Joe decided to skip the service and stay home with his father.

"Ladies and Gentlemen, unfortunately Joe couldn't be with us today. I know he loves me but he just wasn't ready to make this commitment at this time. He tried to back out of the blood test. He tried to back out of putting stamps on the wedding invitations and today he tried to back out of 'til death do us part.' I bear him no resentment, so drink and be merry and let's get to the food."

I never made that speech. No sooner had I learned it than Joe and his father showed up at the church, loose as two geese, laughing up a storm.

For a moment I was disappointed. I had no reason to be thinking about Hershey bars, but I was. I fantasized about melting them and rubbing them all over my face and body during the ceremony.

During the reception I skipped the dinner and went right through the 250 chocolate after-dinner mints I had ordered for the party because I thought they'd be "elegant" to serve. I must have known the "elegance" was all going to wind up in my tummy.

What do you think I was doing while the guests were dancing the hora and the tarantella? I was in the ladies' room stuffing myself with all the roses made of icing. Joe came to look for me. He knocked on the door. "Renée, are you all right?"

"I'm great," I said, licking my fingers so there would be no telltale signs.

Louise Lasser was my maid of honor. She was anorexic figuratively at the time. Before I drove away with Joe I took her aside and said, "Louise, I can't stop eating. What should I do?"

"Think about getting even with someone and don't eat to spite them," she said.

"I can't think of one single person I want to get even with. That's how much stress I'm under."

"Can you help me put on some weight?" Louise asked. "My gown is falling off me."

"Feel sorry for yourself and then make it up with a large pizza with extra cheese."

"I can't think of one single thing I have to feel sorry for myself about," Louise called out to me as I was getting into the car.

"What about envy that I got married and you didn't?" I yelled to her out the car window.

Just as I pulled away, I heard her call out, "Thank you." A few months later she married Woody Allen.

On our honeymoon in Saint Croix a breakfast tray arrived with two different cereals, four fruits and three eggs and bacon.

"I was going to skip breakfast," Joe said.

"That's for me," I said sheepishly.

"Do you have a weight problem?"

"No. I'm so happy, I'm just feeding the good feeling."

5
MARRIED FAT

I did have a weight problem, but I was in denial. I ate when I was guilty that I was happier than my mother, and I ate when I was guilty that I wasn't acting so she wasn't getting fulfillment from me. In other words, any time I was selfish enough to live life for myself, I ate.

By the time we came home from our honeymoon in 1966, Joe and I had each put on 20 pounds.

I went into rehearsal for the George Abbott play, *Agatha Sue*. Mr. Abbott, as he liked to be called, made a big fuss over me, praising me every time I opened my mouth. At out-of-town previews in Boston, he invited me, the author and producer to his room to hear the reviews on television.

"Renée Taylor, as the overweight tootsie, stole the show. George Abbott should forget about the play and just let Miss Taylor come out onstage and do whatever she wants," the reviewer said.

I was thrilled and embarrassed to have that said about me while the play and the other actors were dismissed. George Abbott loved hearing it and had a good laugh about it.

"I guess I'd better go to work so everyone comes up to your standards," he said.

The play closed after one night on Broadway. It was a real treat to work with such a gentleman of the theater, and I had learned to be grateful for my exposure to people of wisdom and experience, like him.

As soon as the play closed, I called Elaine May and said, "How about writing a play for me?"

Elaine said, "You're a writer. Write one for yourself."

"I'm a writer?" Up until then I never thought of myself as one.

"You just need to develop discipline. Write three or four hours a day. And buy a note pad to write on."

In *The Third Ear* I had brought in everything I wrote on scraps of brown paper bags. I carried around all my writing in a shopping bag. I very rarely finished writing anything I started. My biggest problem was putting off the instant gratification of approval until the end. I was like the opera singer who didn't want to wait until the end of the aria for her applause. She wanted it after every little line.

I went away for a week to a motel in Woodstock, New York, to write. Joe came up on Friday night. I showed him what I had written the whole week on a single piece of paper.

"I can't write. I'll never write. I'm a failure."

Now when I speak to people who want to become writers, I tell them to begin by writing out their feelings of inadequacy. Once you express your worst fears, the writing just flows out of you, as it did out of me then. I freed myself by telling myself, "It doesn't have to be good—it just has to be put down on paper." I began to let out all the ideas I had until there was nothing left to write but what was right. At first I wrote scenes, then I put them together in revue form. It was fun, but it was lonely.

"Maybe we should write a play together," I said to Joe.

"We?" Joe said.

"Yeah, let's do it together. It must be easier than doing it alone. We both have the same sense of humor. It'll be funnier than what we see on Broadway. Let's buy a house to write in here. You can come on weekends, and in a couple of months I bet we knock off a play."

"About what?"

"The two funniest people we know. Your father and my mother," I said.

"I don't want to be a writer."

"How about if I give you billing? Taylor and Bologna. Would you want to write with me then?"

"I'll only write with you if you don't put my name on it," he said.

So we bought our first house in Woodstock, and it took us two and a half years to write that play, *Lovers and Other Strangers*. When Joe read it over he said, "Hey, it's good. I want my name on it."

"Read the title page; it's already there."

That two-and-a-half-year period was the only time my weight was consistent. I was constantly one hundred and eighty. During that time Woodstock was having concerts, the flower children were flirting with drugs and I was having what I called my seasonal flare-ups. In summer, I had cantaloupe obsessions. Winter, I had squash overload. Spring, apples. (You wouldn't think anyone could gain on apples, but if you eat them carmeled, you do.) In fall, I overate grapes. I also managed to become a waterholic. The Stillman Diet recommends 2 quarts of water a day, and I became addicted to drinking large pots of water. If there was ever a way for me to become attached to an animal, mineral or vegetable, I did it.

Through it all, Joe stubbornly loved me and my mother, who was spending a great deal of time with us in the country.

"I'm having trouble sleeping, Renée. The sound of the running brook and the crickets is keeping me up," my mother said one night in the kitchen where I was writing. "I keep seeing my past life over and over. Do you think I'll ever be happy? Do you think I'll ever lose weight? Do you think it's too late to be an actress?"

"I don't know, Ma. Look how happy I am writing and just giving up on my weight."

I realized I was keeping myself fat so I wouldn't have more than she did. I acknowledged it to myself, but instead of letting go of it, I held onto it to protect me. By being fat I was showing my mother I was not to be envied. I was her clone, not a threatening rival.

Joe had quit his job with the advertising agency to spend full time writing the final draft of our play with me. He wanted to direct it, but decided to wait until the next one since we wanted Charles Grodin to direct because he was so talented and objective. He came up on weekends to talk over suggested rewrites of the play. One weekend, he brought Simon and Garfunkel, and they sang to us and we read them some of our material.

The tent dress was in fashion, and I remember thinking how lucky I was that it was in style when I went to see Harold Prince about producing *Lovers*. He was all tied up in other projects, but after he read it he gave me $500 as our first investor. He suggested a young producer, Stephanie Sills, for our play. I had intended to play all the female parts in *Lovers*, but Stephanie said that as its co-author I would be making myself too vulnerable, so I only did one part. Years later, many well-known actors and actresses toured the country, each playing all the male and female parts as a tour de force.

The night before we went into rehearsal, we decided to have a baby right away. The play meant so much to us that our identity was all wrapped up in it.

"Our life has to be more important. Our baby has to be the greatest thing we create." We both agreed. It was a miracle—on our first try I got pregnant.

At rehearsal, Charles Grodin asked my mother to make a speech to the cast.

"This is a wonderful play. You are all wonderful. Bobby Alto, Candy Azzara, Mary Claire Costello, Richard Castellano, Ron Carey, Zohra Lampert, Marvin Lichteman, Gerald S. O'Loughlin, Dick Van Patten. And my daughter, Renée. The world is waiting for you. Go forth and be brilliant," my mother said.

I was in the audience, munching on the Astronauts' Fat Wars Diet.

* * *

Astronauts' Fat Wars Diet

Breakfast: 1 serving of fruit
2 ounces of lean meat
1 piece of toast with 1 teaspoon margarine
1 cup of skim milk
Black coffee or tea

Lunch: 4 ounces of lean meat or poultry
Broccoli
1 serving of fruit
Black coffee or tea

Dinner: 4 ounces of lean meat or poultry
1 cup of green peas or 1 biscuit
1 serving of fruit
Black coffee or tea

Snack: 1 cup of milk
1 piece of fruit

I had three months until our opening in New York to lose 50 pounds. I cut it close—I just made it. We tried out in Detroit and Chicago, and by the time we got back to New York, I weighed 135 and was three months pregnant.

When I got pregnant, I was a heavy smoker—three packs a day. I went to a famous naturopath, Dr. Walters.

"Could you give me something to help me cut down? I can't quit cold turkey," I said.

"Take the end of your cigarette and insert it in your rectum."

"Uh-huh."

"Then light the other end."

"Uh-huh."

"Then inhale deeply and by the time you finish that cigarette you'll cut down," said Dr. Walters.

"Uh-huh," I said.

It wasn't until I was out of his office that I understood what he was really telling me. What a fool I was to just cut down when I would hurt the baby and myself by not giving it up altogether. I threw away my pack of cigarettes, and that night I woke up in the middle of the night craving a smoke. I got furious that I was hooked on cigarettes, and that helped me quit. Backstage in Chicago I had met the president of the cigarette company that manufactured my brand. When I offered him a cigarette, he said, "I don't smoke. I'm allergic to it." Thinking about that helped me kill my smoking habit too.

In Detroit, David Susskind and Bob Precht came to see the play and wanted to buy it as a movie.

"Five hundred thousand dollars is the price," a voice told him in our dressing room.

"Who are you?" David Susskind asked the voice.

"I'm her mother. Shall I read you what *Variety* said about this play? And I quote: 'It's today. It's pithy, it's trenchant.' That's why it's worth $500,000."

We all laughed, but we sold it for more than half that amount before the play even opened on Broadway. We were so thrilled to be authors that we would have been happy to sell it for very little. But by then we had a well-known lawyer, Bella Linden, an important business manager, Marty Bregman, and a big agent, Paul Rosen, and with their help we were *rich* overnight.

Rich and pregnant and acting on Broadway in my own play. I couldn't imagine having anything more in life. Joe and I and Charles Grodin and the whole cast were filled with great expectations that our play would last forever. Why not? The audience never stopped laughing from beginning to end. Sometimes the laughs lasted for thirty seconds—and that's a long, hearty laugh. We sat elated at the party upstairs at Sardi's until we heard the first review on television.

"A thing opened on Broadway tonight that was Neanderthal Theater," said the reviewer.

"That can't be our play he's talking about. He must have been at another theater," I said.

But then we heard him say *"Lovers and Other Strangers."* That was my first glimpse of how devastating life in the theater could be. Was I glad I was having my baby!

The next television review was a rave, and so was the *New York Times* review. Clive Barnes said we were "comedy geniuses." I didn't care what happened after that. I was only modestly praised as an actress, but I was on such a high because I'd been discovered as a writer that I hardly noticed.

It's lucky that I didn't care, because we closed after three months. But not before Joe made his acting debut on Broadway. One of the actors, Gerald S. O'Loughlin, was offered a movie part and we had to replace him. I said, "What about Joe? He'd be perfect. He was so funny at all the backers' auditions. Audiences will eat him up."

"Won't he be too nervous to go on in four days?" Stephanie the producer asked.

"Not at all. He acted in college shows. He's raring to go."

It wasn't until *after* I had convinced her he could step right in without a hitch that I turned to Joe and asked him, "What do you think, Joe? Can you do it?"

He was a natural. He loved being up there and it came through in his work. His father was in the audience, cheering him on. He came backstage and winked at Richard Castellano. "I know what you're doing. You're playing me," Mr. Bologna told Richard. To Joe he said, "Think about being an actor. You're good."

After the show Joe and I sat with Tony Bologna at the Italian restaurant next door and tried to figure out how to save the play. "I'm making all my shoe-shine customers buy tickets. That'll keep it going for a month anyway," he said.

He had shined shoes to put Joe through Brown University. Their pride in each other was mutual. I watched his father walk away from us, windbreaker collar turned up, porkpie hat down over his forehead, baggy pants rolled up, and I was proud of him too.

After three months, we had to get out of the theater. It was an interrun booking and we couldn't afford to move, so the play closed.

We went to Woodstock to write the screenplay for *Lovers and Other Strangers,* and a weird thing happened. I always assumed I would be in the movie. I hadn't put it in my contract, I just assumed it. But they had no intention of giving me my own part, the one I had written for myself. So I had no recourse but to gain more weight. Since I was pregnant, I could disguise it. I put on 60 pounds. "It'll be a huge baby—I can tell," I kept saying.

We were on our first trip to Italy. I was eating everything in sight. Only when the Italian doctor in Positano said, "If you lose this baby, you can have another one," did we decide to come back to the States for the birth. Gabriel weighed 5 pounds, 4 ounces when he was born. Was I embarrassed that the extra 50 pounds was all fat!

I had natural childbirth, and Joe held my hand and whispered sweet words of encouragement to me and the baby. As soon as Gabriel was handed to me I ordered a steak and went on Jack LaLanne's High Protein Diet.

Jack LaLanne's High Protein Diet

Breakfast: ½ grapefruit
2 eggs
Lunch: ½ grapefruit
2 eggs
Dinner: 2 eggs
Steak

Elaine May wrote a part for me in a movie she was directing, *A New Leaf,* with Walter Matthau. Whenever Gabriel cried because it was feeding time, Elaine called "Cut" and I breast-fed Gabriel in a trailer. The six months of breast-feeding were happy for me. My pediatrician and my obstetrician both told me that breast-feeding kept your weight in control. The

LaLanne Diet was a bore, but it certainly helped too. By the end of it, I wouldn't eat another egg if you paid me.

To get over the heartbreak of my not being in the movie of *Lovers and Other Strangers*, I quickly began writing another movie, with the stipulation I had to be in it. It was about a girl from the moment of her conception, and all the men in her life until she meets the right one. It was called *Myrna Gold and the Lost Sailor*. Joe read it and loved it. "Why not make it about him and all the women in his life, beginning at his conception too, and I'll write it with you," Joe said.

That idea became *Made for Each Other*. Just as we were finished writing it, the movie *Lovers and Other Strangers* opened in New York. I woke up one morning in Woodstock to the sound of Tony Bologna's voice.

"Josie, Josie," he called to his wife. "We got four stars in the *Daily News*."

We were ecstatic that our screenplay got such a reception. The reviews all over the country were raves, and the picture made a lot of money, which could only help us get *Made for Each Other* produced. I was having trouble getting it made with just me starring in it. Almost all the studios wanted to make the picture, but if I was to be in it, they wanted a bigger name in the leading role opposite me. It looked like it would take a Brando or a Redford to satisfy them.

Now there was another trauma. Joe's father had an accident. He blacked out and fell in his kitchen, breaking his spine. In the hospital, he sent for me.

"How come I was so mean to you and you never told me to take a walk?"

"Because I love you. At first, I loved you just because you were Joe's father. But now I love you because you're you."

"You know, I didn't like your looks when I met you, but in case you're interested you've gotten much prettier."

"Thank you for saying that."

"Do me a favor. Put Joe in your movie. I think he'll make a heck of an actor."

"Are you sure? I like being the only actor in the family," I said, not taking it seriously yet.

Tony chuckled softly. That was the last time I ever saw him. I told Joe what his father had said. He listened quietly without saying anything. A few weeks later we were driving to Woodstock and talking about Gabriel's colic. Suddenly, Joe blurted out, "I have to be in *Made for Each Other* with you."

"But Joe, we'll never get it done."

"I lived it. I felt it. I don't want anyone acting out our love story with you but me," he said. "You've got to help me do it with you."

"Oh, boy." Now I was taking it seriously.

Now began my all-day pizza diet.

Renée's Pizza Diet

Breakfast: Pizza with extra cheese
Lunch: Pizza with pepperoni
Dinner: Pizza with extra cheese, pepperoni, anchovies and mushrooms

I read in the Sunday *New York Times* about a primal scream group run by Dr. Daniel Casriel. Joe and I had written a scene into the movie in which the two main characters meet during emergency group therapy. I thought it would be a good idea to observe what really took place at a group encounter session. Once we were there, I thought: Forget about observing—I wanted to participate. I told the group I had a real problem with Joe being in the movie with me because I had spent ten years becoming an actress and I didn't want to share the experience when I deserved to have it alone. Joe was a successful commercial director, wasn't that enough for him?

"I don't want anyone saying 'I love you' to you on the screen but me," Joe said. "Anyway, I wrote my part for me. It was always my intention to play it, and now I want what's mine."

That Joe always wanted to be an actor was a big shock to me, but I couldn't say no, because I loved him and I didn't want to be selfish. I also appreciated his natural talent. I was happy that he was going after what he wanted, and that he felt entitled to get it. I thought it was great. What upset me was that so much of my identity was in my acting, and I didn't want to share any more of it than I already did with my mother. I understood his feelings and mine, but it took me twenty years to get over Joe's becoming an actor.

Our friend Fred Levinson and his partner, Bob Bean, who finally directed the movie, sent it to Twentieth Century–Fox. Richard Zanuck, the vice-president, read the script, and our new agent, Larry Auerbach, from the William Morris agency, told us Zanuck wanted to talk us into selling it to the studio. Joe and I decided, since I was the professional actor, I should go alone and plead the case for both of us to act in the movie. I remember my nose was running the day of the appointment. At first I thought of canceling—how could I talk them into my being one of the stars of the picture when I didn't look like one? Then I decided that would be part of my argument.

Richard Zanuck was a handsome young man. He sat on a high, thronelike chair. I was shown to a low chair. I wondered why. Then I realized he was a short man and the seating was designed to make him seem much bigger. I kept sitting up taller and taller in my chair so I could look into his eyes as an equal. When I realized it was impossible, I folded my legs under me and sat on them.

"You're an experienced actress, but it's best to have a big name in the movie. Don't you think the picture would make more money if Elizabeth Taylor played the part? Don't you think it might be an even better picture if Barbra Streisand played it?" he asked very reasonably.

"Maybe. But it's irrelevant."

"Why is it irrelevant?"

"Because I wrote it, and if I am not for myself, who will be?" I said, quoting from Hillel. "You should appreciate my feeling. I heard that your father asked you to step aside as head of the studio but you had a higher calling from your conscience. I'm a plain-looking girl with a cold. That's how the part should be played."

"I'm starting to get your point of view."

"It gets worse," I said. "My husband, Joe, wants to play the man's part, and he's not only *not* a name, he's not even an experienced actor."

"You must be joking. I can't even consider that."

"I appreciate your honesty and the speediness of your reply. However, we want to make a screen test for you at our own expense. If you don't like it, no hard feelings. If you do—well anyhow, it's the only way we'll sell the picture."

"We're going to test for the movie," I told Joe excitedly when I got home.

"What happened to give you so much courage?"

"I felt I had nothing so I had nothing to lose."

That way of looking at things had always worked for me before. This time it worked again.

Joe and I did an hour's worth of scenes from the movie. Bob Bean directed us to be very funny and loving with each other. When we sat and looked at the test in the screening room, we knew the picture would be done, if not by Zanuck at Twentieth, by somebody. Zanuck said yes. We were on our way to having our dream. Then my mother wanted to play *her* own part in the movie. Bob, the director, wanted Helen Verbit, who was a hilarious professional actress.

"Go to acting school, Ma, and I'll insist he read you for the part," I said.

"I've been studying with Bill Hickey for six months," she answered.

I was so proud of her.

I said, "Let's write a new part for her in the picture, Joe," and we did. We didn't tell Bob it was my mother. We just brought her in with the other actors when it was time to do the scene. She was very feisty in the group scene, telling Joe, "Keep your stupid mouth shut."

Making the movie was such an intense experience that it

was hard to go back to everyday life. Joe, my mother and I became fruitarians during the shoot. We had an exercise trainer who lived on fruit and berries for carbohydrates and nuts for protein, and we exercised hard with him at 4:30 A.M. every morning and ate our meals at his house.

John Hill's Berry Diet

Breakfast: Raspberries and almonds
Lunch: Bananas, dates, raisins
Dinner: Spaghetti
Strawberries and goat's milk

John Hill looked forty but he was in his early sixties. I didn't realize my mother was in love with him until she cried upon hearing that he was going to marry a younger woman. Joe and I both put our arms around her and comforted her.

"Renée, I really feel Joe loves me. He's the first man since your father who ever cared that deeply for me," my mother confided to me.

"There will be others, Mother. You'll see. Now that you're an actress, you'll have a lot more opportunities to meet them too."

While we were waiting for *Made for Each Other* to be released, we were nominated for an Academy Award for the screenplay for *Lovers and Other Strangers*.

I went on a crash diet before I went to the Awards.

The Nova Scotia Smoked Salmon Diet

Breakfast: 4 ounces Nova Scotia smoked salmon, capers, onions
Lunch: 4 ounces Nova Scotia smoked salmon, capers, onions
Dinner: Diced lobster or shrimp
Salad

In the lobby of the Pantages Theater, all the movie stars paraded past me. I was so tongue-tied that when Anthony Quinn remembered me from a Broadway audition and I introduced Joe to him, I couldn't remember Joe's last name.

"This is my husband, Joe Bolo—, Bolo—."

"—gna," Joe added.

Joe was cool as a cucumber. He only got excited when he met someone from the Mets or the New York Yankees.

Sitting in the audience, I was sure that if God had let us be nominated on our first movie it was a sign we would win too. After all, it had cost a fortune for my gown and Joe's tux and our air fare. When the name Ring Lardner, Jr., was announced for best screenplay for *M*A*S*H,* I said, "I never heard of him. Who is that?"

"Me," said the man rising up out of the seat next to me.

When we got back home to New York, my mother was waiting for me. "Renée, I got all dressed up to watch the Awards. I was so nervous I ate a whole fruitcake. Could I have your nomination award? I'd like to keep it to look at."

"No, Mother," I said. "I can't part with it. It means too much to me."

"You have two, Renée, counting Joe's. I'd like to feel a small part of it belongs to me."

"Please don't ask me, Mother."

Later I would be very sorry that I felt so possessive about my accomplishment that I couldn't give it to her.

Made for Each Other opened in New York in 1972 to sensational reviews. *Photoplay* magazine picked Joe as the most promising star. Judith Crist said I was a combination of Marilyn Monroe and Laurence Olivier. We were on the cover of *New York* magazine. At the premiere, Gabriel tried to talk to me up on the screen. I remember thinking, I am at the peak of my life experience.

Then something totally unexpected happened. Every time the telephone rang it was someone offering Joe, instead of me, a starring role in another movie.

I was crushed. "Can't you be sad for you and happy for me?" Joe asked.

"I would if I could, but I can't."

"Okay," he said emphatically. "Then we'll both be sad."

Immediately I called my mother to share the pain and to tell her how understanding Joe was. There was no answer. A few hours later I got scared and took a cab to her apartment. There was no answer. I broke the door down, and found her body on the floor. She'd had a heart attack the night before and died.

"Ma, I'm sorry I didn't give you my award," I told her. I was only glad I hadn't told her that all the calls were for Joe—I would have thought that had killed her. At least she died thinking I was on my way to being a big star. Or did that idea kill her—that it was to be me and not her? Was she punishing herself because she had failed to fulfill her own secret dream of being an actress? Whatever caused her heart attack, her loss was unbearable to me. I judged myself guilty on so many counts, most of all that I had a happier marriage than she did. I had all these reasons to get fat again, and I went into a deep mourning.

During the time right after my mother's death, *Last of the Red Hot Lovers*, a movie I had done with Alan Arkin, was released, and with Joe I co-wrote *Acts of Love and Other Comedies* for Marlo Thomas. We won an Emmy for it. I also did a television series for Jimmy Coco, *Calucci's Department*, and a television special for Joe and me, *Paradise*, for which we were nominated for a Writers Guild Award.

In spite of all this success, my lesser recognition as an actress, combined with the death of my mother, affected me like a double whammy. My coping mechanism broke. The thermostat that told my stomach when it was full stopped working. Food was my comforter and my best friend. I had such an intimate relationship with it that we were inseparable. I shopped for it, I cooked it, I served it, I ate it round the clock.

Then, when it was time for Gabriel to start kindergarten,

That's me in the carriage, looking like I'm going to cry, and my darling mother Frieda Silverstein posing 1930s-style.

My chubby beginnings.

I made Perry Como laugh on his show, one of my first big breaks.
(Photo courtesy of The National Broadcasting Co. Inc.)

With Jerry Lewis in my first movie, *The Errand Boy*.
(Photo courtesy of Paramount Pictures)

Here I am trying to be a femme fatale in a B movie, *The Mugger*.
(Photo courtesy of United Artists)

Alan Arkin "seduced" me in *Last of the Red Hot Lovers*.
(Photo courtesy of Paramount Pictures)

I worked with Frank Sinatra and Jack Klugman in *The Detective*.
(Photo courtesy of 20th Century-Fox)

 The MGM press release on this publicity shot said, "Renée Taylor, an award-winning writer in real life, plays the part Katharine Hepburn first created as Tess Harding, the award-winning writer in *Woman of the Year.*" Was I impressed!
(Photo courtesy of MGM)

My Rita Hayworth impression from *Made for Each Other.*
(Renée Taylor's photo courtesy of 20th Century-Fox. Rita Hayworth's photo courtesy of Columbia Pictures)

Here's me and Joe in a publicity still for *Woman of the Year*. You can see I loved wearing that hat, and I always wanted the life that went with it.
(Photo courtesy of MGM)

Me and Joe at Marlo Thomas's house for an ERA frundraiser.
I was one of the hostesses.
(Photo by Stan Adams)

With Joe and our son Gabriel on last year's Christmas card.
(Photo by Suzanne Murphy, courtesy of the Los Angeles Times)

Joe said to me, "I love you fat. I love you thin. But most of all, I love you thin. Lose some weight."

"Mind your own business. You were fat when I met you and it was okay for me."

"We're moving to Hollywood. Do you know what they do to fat people there? They stone them. I'm just preparing you for what's in store for you."

"I can't diet while I'm still in mourning for my mother."

"No one loved Frieda more than me," Joe said. "But after a year and a half, crying night and day, your mourning is boring."

"Boring? I can never forgive you for calling my pain boring. I want a divorce."

The next day when I woke up I looked in the mirror at the sad expression on my face.

"Renée, I hope this doesn't hurt your feelings, but your pain is boring me too. Do something about it," I told myself.

First, I put a headstone on my mother's grave, with a large five-pointed dressing-room star that said "You are loved" inside it. "Don't think me disloyal, Mother, but it's time to say goodbye. I'll never forget you," I told her.

Then I got Rolfed and I had my ears stapled by an acupuncturist so I would lose my appetite. Finally, I went gung ho on the Army–Air Force Diet.

Army–Air Force Diet

Breakfast: 2 eggs, scrambled
½ cup fresh strawberries
Grilled ham
½ slice white toast
Coffee or tea

Lunch: 2 thick lamb chops
Salad
Melon
Coffee

Dinner: (Before dinner, Scotch and soda;
during dinner, 3 glasses of wine)
Roast pork
Mushrooms and cheese
Buttered asparagus
Tossed salad
Tangerine
(After dinner, brandy)

It took me three and a half months to lose 45 pounds. During that time, Joe was becoming a sex symbol. The world agreed with my taste, and I was starting to view it as a compliment. And a blessing. I was ready to take on Hollywood.

6

BEVERLY HILLS FAT

When we first arrived in Hollywood in 1974, we drove from the airport singing "We're in the Money." We had sold our house in Woodstock and we thought we were rich. That is, until we saw what our money would buy in Hollywood. Not much. So we decided to rent. Almost every house in Beverly Hills has a history of some movie star who lived there—it's really just a small town with big houses. I was thrilled just to visit some of them, let alone live in them.

First we moved into Carole Lombard's old house. The white bedroom and bath were all mirrored and so was the ceiling. It was the first time I had seen bottled spring water on tap, and I thought that's what being rich must be. The rent was very high for Joe and me, but the garden had the most unusual assortment of flowers and fruits growing in it (strawberries, avocados, oranges, lemons and figs), so I told Joe, "Look how much money we'll save on fruit and flowers." Actually, what saved us the most money was the mirrored bedroom and bath. When we saw how fat we were from every angle, we weren't too hungry.

All our friends and relatives wanted to visit us in Beverly Hills. They were star struck too. We once had twenty-two sleeping at our house, including six people and their dog who were neighbors of my sister-in-law, who came cross-country in their station wagon to go to Disneyland and stopped by late at night to say hello, plus four people and their dog who were having their house painted and they couldn't stand the fumes. When I jokingly said, "The only place we can put you up is in the bathtubs," they said, "We'll take it."

The whole neighborhood was filled with the idols of my childhood. Down the block was Lucille Ball. Every day her fans went through her garbage in the alley—not to steal it, to know what she ate.

"Look, Shirley, she had egg rolls last night, and boysenberry ice cream," I heard one woman tell her friend.

The only star's food I ever touched belonged to Fred Astaire. When he left the Beverly Hills Coffee Shop one day, I noticed he had left two packages of Ry-Krisps on his plate.

"You want one of Fred Astaire's Ry-Krisps?" I asked Joe.

"I'm full."

"I mean to keep, not to eat," I said, slipping both packages in my pocket. Years later when I met Fred I said, "I have your Ry-Krisp crumbs." He smiled politely and pretended I was telling him something normal.

Just about everybody in the neighborhood had a great body. I saw them every morning around 6:00 A.M., jogging on the Beverly Hills track. Not only were their bodies good, but they wore matching ensembles. On my first run around the park I felt that my body wasn't good enough to be seen. I thought I'd better get in shape privately before I got in shape publicly. Charlton Heston passed me, and he yelled, "Run, run."

"I am running," I yelled back. I was obviously not fast enough for him.

My next-door neighbor was a very big star, but I noticed one day that she had pulled down all her window shades. Her picture had been printed in the *Enquirer*, and they called her the worst thing you could call an actress in Hollywood. Not an adulteress, not even over forty. The headline over her photograph read: *Overweight*.

I ran into her one day at Premier Market, where all the stars shop. My mother-in-law and I were laughing at the fruit prices. Eight dollars for a box of raspberries. My neighbor was filling her cart with them.

"Are you freezing them?" my mother-in-law asked. "Because they're much cheaper at Grand Union."

"No," my neighbor said, lowering her dark glasses and whispering. "I'm on the Raspberry Diet. Six boxes a day for eight days. Then raspberry juice for eight days."

"Poor thing," my mother-in-law said to me when she left. "She'd have to eat raspberries for a year and it still wouldn't make a dent in her fat."

I guess the raspberries didn't work, because in three weeks she had her jaws wired shut. A few nights later she got desperate for solid food and came over to our house at midnight to borrow our tools.

"What do you need wire cutters for?" I asked.

She pointed to her mouth.

"Oh, my God, I heard that wiring your jaw only works if you wire your nose too," I said. I knew what a mess she was going to make of her jaw and was trying to make light of it.

She didn't even chuckle. She just took the cutters and left. I was grateful she didn't unwire herself in front of me—I would have fainted.

A few days later my fat movie-star friend from next door told me her story. She had just gotten a divorce from another very famous movie star who was quite a lover on screen and off. They met at the Bistro over goose pâté. They became binge buddies. They even incorporated food into their sex, smothering themselves with whipped cream. It was very sensual. Then one day she came home early from the set and caught him in their sunken bathtub filled with lime Jell-O and another woman. He moved out that day.

"Here's all he left me with," she said, lifting up her sweat shirt and showing me her seven rolls of fat.

Gabriel was starting kindergarten, and if there ever was a time in my life to go Hollywood, this was it. We were there because we'd been asked by MGM to remake *Woman of the*

Year for television. Originally, it had starred Katharine Hepburn and Spencer Tracy, and they were perfect in it. "What part would I play?" I asked Fred Silverman, president of CBS.

"Katharine Hepburn's part."

"Oh, I can't be better than her."

"Just be yourself," he said.

Be yourself? That sounded easy. But I was scared that "myself" wasn't enough.

Like my parents before me, I always felt like an outsider who wants to be an insider, but now I was on the inside playing the part of someone even more inside. Gene Kelly was suggested by the studio to direct the movie, and he met with us at our new, even-fancier-than-Lombard's house. It was Greta Garbo's old house. I saw the original lease she signed, and in the blank where her age should be written in she wrote a question mark.

We needed a larger house for all our friends and relatives from the Bronx and Brooklyn who came out to visit. Most of them couldn't afford a hotel, and anyway it was more fun having them stay in an old Hollywood mansion with us. MGM gave us expense money to pay for the house. We could have pocketed it and lived in an apartment hotel like other actors from the East Coast, but we wanted the fun of the life of luxury.

It was mostly me, I confess. "Just once, let's live like Garbo lived," I said to Joe. I was lying, because once I moved in I never wanted to leave. Even her wallpaper was great. It was real white silk embossed with a red velvet fleur-de-lis. The pool had sprinklers, so that while you swam across it you were cooled off by fresh water spraying on your face. The closet doors were made of glass, so you could see your clothes and pull them out toward you like in a clothing store. Garbo had lived there with Gaylord Hauser, the health-food expert, and they lived on raw fruits and vegetables, so there was no real kitchen in the house. All they needed was a sink to wash the vegetables. I found cases of blackstrap molasses in the garage.

Hauser had said in his book, *Look Younger, Live Longer,* that it would add five youthful years to your life, turn gray hair back to its normal color and even grow hair on your head when it was in short supply.

Living in Garbo's house, I felt I had to go on the diet Gayelord Hauser prescribed for her. Maybe some of her looks would rub off on me. After a while, I began to talk like Ninotchka.

Greta Garbo's Diet

Breakfast: Bulgarian yogurt with blackstrap molasses
Lunch: Tomato soup with celery-flavored brewer's yeast
Dinner: Wild-rice nutburgers

There were orange trees in the backyard, and the Mexican gardener told me that Garbo would run through the garden barefoot and naked except for two oranges held in place under her mink coat. She would play peekaboo, flashing for Gayelord Hauser. The oranges would drop out of her coat, and she would laugh and run away, and Gayelord would chase her, laughing too. I loved hearing that the great Garbo could be silly. We had a young French nursemaid, and when I told her the story, she said, "Who's Greta Garbo?" That hurt me as much as if it had been me she was talking about.

I bought clothes that I thought Garbo would wear. Victorian, yet sexy. Sparse, yet frilly. I tried hard to look the way she looked in *Camille*.

I was so happy, I couldn't help thinking how my mother would have been thrilled to live there with us too. Joe and I were invited to a costume party and a séance on Halloween at the Friars Club in Beverly Hills. I went, hoping I could wake my mother's spirit and bring her back to the Garbo house with me. All the Friars Club members were there—Red Buttons, George Burns, Danny Thomas, Buddy Hackett, Don Rickles.

At the party, Milton Berle asked me, "Who are you supposed to be?"

"Garbo."

"In what movie?"

"*Anna Karenina.* The last scene, just before she threw herself under the train."

He laughed, thinking I was joking. I was serious.

At the séance, all of them had visits from their departed friends and relatives. Al Jolson appeared to Milton Berle. I sat there all night, and I couldn't understand why my mother hadn't shown up in Hollywood, her favorite place. I decided she preferred being in Heaven giving advice to real movie stars. Clark Gable and Joan Crawford.

There I was, a girl from the Bronx married to a guy from Brooklyn, and we had a French cook, an upstairs maid, a downstairs maid and a chauffeur. We really put on the dog.

Into all of this came Gene Kelly to meet with us about *Woman of the Year.* Just as he was saying to Joe, "What I loved about Renée in *Made for Each Other* is she's so natural. She hasn't a phony thing about her," I made a grand entrance down the long staircase wearing a long satin and marabou dressing gown. "Are you being serious?" he asked, with a twinkle in his eye.

"Don't you think I'm the glamorous type?"

"No. But don't forget, I've seen them all."

Shortly afterward, Gene Kelly quit. He thought I was patterning myself too much after Katharine Hepburn. He was right. I was given bad advice—by myself. My logic was that maybe I hadn't been glamorous enough in *Made for Each Other,* or sexy enough in *Last of the Red Hot Lovers.* Now I would be both. I had such a good time making the movie it was almost worth the nervous breakdown that came afterward. Almost.

Moss Mabry designed my wardrobe. He had worked with Lana Turner and Rita Hayworth, and he taught me all sorts of things about clothes that I never knew.

"Pipe a chiffon gown with satin because it looks so nice

near your skin." "Use only black sable for the collar of a long, black, silk-velvet coat." "Little sprigs of baby's breath tucked in each curl of your hair in an upsweep is elegant."

MGM had a full-length portrait of me painted for one scene in the movie. I wrote it into the script because all the movie stars had one over the fireplace in their houses. When Harris Cattleman, the studio head, asked me if it was necessary for the movie (we were overbudget, and the painter wanted $3,000), I wanted it so badly I said, "Without the portrait the whole movie won't work."

My wardrobe cost $15,000. It looked like a million. Harris said, "If you finish the movie on schedule, we'll give you your wardrobe as a present."

I pushed myself and Joe to make the schedule. Moss Mabry told me to lose fifteen more pounds. He gave me the diet that Rita Hayworth used before filming *Gilda*, and Marilyn Monroe used before filming *Bus Stop*. It's called:

The Movie Star's Emergency Diet

To 2 quarts of warm water add: 1 teaspoon sea salt, 1 tablespoon maple syrup, 2 tablespoons lemon juice, dash of cayenne pepper.

Each day, drink ten glasses. You lose a pound a day for fifteen days.

It is the worst, but in an emergency you won't mind because it works. I went from size eight to size four. I was thinner than I'd ever been. My costumes for the movie hung loose. I had the studio dressmaker, Frances Spencer, take them all in until they were skintight.

"Are you sure you want to do this?" Frances asked. "It will mean that you can never gain an ounce."

"Exactly. That's a little psychological trick I'm using to keep myself thin forever. I'm throwing out all my old clothes, and I'm just keeping the movie clothes. I won't be able to gain because I won't have a thing to wear."

(That's a little psychological trick you can forget about ever trying. When the movie ended in disaster, I blew up like a blimp, and because I had nothing that fit me, I hid in the house all day in the same old sweat clothes. I felt like too much of a jerk to buy new fat women's clothes.)

During my wardrobe fittings for *Woman of the Year*, I was madly in love with myself as a size four. I walked differently, with little baby steps, sashaying my hips back and forth. I no longer viewed myself as a fat person. I was *someone* who happened to be the thinnest person in the whole world. It was a feeling worth dying for.

William Tuttle did the makeup tests for the movie. He gave me Joan Crawford's eyebrows, Marilyn Monroe's doe eyes, Kathryn Grayson's mouth and Gene Tierney's cheekbones. He had done the makeup for all these stars, and he taught me all their little beauty tricks. After one of the tests he said, "Have you thought about shaving your nose?"

"I thought we did."

"I don't mean with makeup, with a knife. I have a friend who's done practically everyone's nose in Hollywood." He even mentioned a superstar's name.

"I didn't know she had her nose fixed."

"Three times."

"Okay," I said. "Let's go."

We went to see this famous plastic surgeon the following week. He drew a picture of how I'd look after the operation. It wasn't anything like me.

"I don't know," I said. "I kind of like my own nose, bumpy as it is." (I was hit on the nose with a baseball when I was seven.)

"Okay," he said. "Keep the nose, but do the eyes and the chin."

"I think I have nice eyes."

"Now, sure, but in five years it all droops. You'll have to do something about the deep lines in your forehead and around your mouth. A scraping and a peeling won't be enough. I could pull back the skin on your hands too."

"My hands? People are doing their hands?"

"And the feet. Age shows up there too, and your thighs. Why not lift them?"

"Are you suggesting all this for beauty or for youthfulness?"

"Neither. This is not vanity. In your case, I'm suggesting for you what's *necessary*."

I was catatonic. "Uh, I'll have to discuss it with my husband."

"Well, don't take too long. I'm booked up a year in advance."

"Oh, well, that lets me out. I need it right away. I start a movie in three weeks." I was so relieved to get out of it that when I got home I had a big cry.

"Joe, I'm falling apart."

"Renée, please promise me you won't do anything to change your looks. They might botch it."

The night of the *Woman of the Year* screening at MGM, I was terribly excited. I invited all my friends. I had seen the rushes and thought I never looked prettier. I kept wanting to make my part funnier, but everyone had gotten caught up in how sophisticated I looked. Joe will be the funny one, said the studio head, the network chief and my agent. You just stand there and look lovely. In my wildest dreams I was not prepared for what happened. I expected a triumph, to be discovered as Carole Lombard and Greta Garbo rolled into one. Standing in the back of the theater, I noticed that people were walking out before the picture was over. First one by one, then two by two. When you remake a classic, it has to be better. This wasn't as good. It was, to be kind, conventional.

On his way out of the theater, Carl Reiner said to me, "What did you want to do that for?"

Gene Wilder said, "Other people do this sort of thing much better."

Joe, who's always as great during a disaster as he is with a success, wasn't as devastated as I was.

"Well, I guess from now on we'll have to perform in our other style," he said as a joke.

But I threw myself face down on the bearskin rug in a spread-eagle position and sobbed, "I'm finished, Joe. I'll never come back from this one. I'll never do better than this, and they don't like this."

But that was only the beginning of my troubles. The chairman of the board of the studio and my agent wouldn't answer my calls, and I'd heard that the network chief said he'd like to kill me. That's how much he hated the movie.

Then my agent called. Usually each year he would ask us to sign again for the new year. Now, when I answered the phone he asked to speak to Joe.

"It's Renée."

"I know," he said. "I'd just like to have Joe as a client. You've been holding him back in his career. By forcing him to work in this bomb with you, you really hurt his reputation." He blamed me for the failure of the movie even though Joe was as bland in the film as I was. Everyone in Hollywood blamed me. I put down the phone, too stunned to speak.

"Joe, have I been holding you back?"

"How dare he say that to you! I'm leaving him too." (He did and we both didn't work for a year.)

One night the chairman of the board of the studio gave his annual party. A friend called us and asked if he could go in our car since his was being fixed.

"I didn't know there was a party," I said. Then, to cover my embarrassment, "I'm sure it's just an oversight. We'll be invited."

"I'm sure you will," he said. "I'll call you right back."

A few minutes later he called back. "It's no oversight. You weren't invited. I feel so bad that I told you about the party."

"Don't be silly," I said. "I'll get even."

"How?"

"I'll get fat," I said jokingly. But then I thought, I do have one of the all-time best reasons to be fat: to get revenge on Hollywood's God and Goddess: Muscular and Underweight.

The God of Muscular in Hollywood is personified by a superstar known for his macho muscles. According to one of my exercise teachers, he is on thyroid pills and steroids and every now and then needs to go on a kidney machine to breathe.

The Goddess of Underweight in Hollywood is personified by a superstar known for her blond frailty, yet she manages to eat all her favorite junk food. When I ran into her on line at Pinky's, eating her second double chili hot dog, I asked her, "What diet are you on that you can pig out like this and be a size two?"

She whispered to me, "Renée, the secret happens after your meal. You take two fingers . . ." (She's a practicing bulimic.)

I was crazy to gain weight when I had worked so hard to lose it for the movie, but gaining turned me on too. I rarely saw a fat person in Beverly Hills, where it's considered a sin to be fat. I had seen the studio head back up from an obese woman like Dracula from the cross.

My next-door neighbor cried to me that when she weighed 112 pounds she was on the A List for Hollywood parties. When her weight went up to 135 pounds she was on the B List, and now that her weight was 178 she was off the C List. When she called the press agent handling the Academy Awards party at Spago's, to confirm her invitation, he said her name was not on the list. My friend said, "How come? I've gone every year for ten years."

The press agent said, "I'll be honest with you. Our host and hostess will be taking photographs with all the guests, and they've asked that any celebrity who is 20 pounds or more overweight is not to be included."

I told her, "It's nothing personal. It's the 'weight of life' in Hollywood." Fat threatens them more than *poor*. "If two Rolls-Royces pull up at a Beverly Hills party," Chuck of Chuck's Valet Parking said, "I'll always open the thinner driver's door first. They are the 'somebodies.'"

Knowing how cruel Hollywood could be to fatties, why did I deliberately set out to get fat? I certainly wasn't appreciated for getting svelte and working hard to look as pretty and sexy as I could. I guess I secretly thought, as a lot of fat people do, that if I ever did get thin people would come running out of their houses, ecstatic about how I looked. Now that I finally looked great and no one cared, something snapped inside my head. I would blow up like a Goodyear blimp, and that would get a rise out of Hollywood. My mischievousness had gone perverse, and I started a binge to end all binges. If you're ever in the mood to go to hell with yourself, here's what to overeat at what restaurant.

Great Hollywood Binge

Golden Caviar with Blini and Sour Cream—*Bistro Gardens*
Walnut Pâté—*Mortimer's*
Deviled Beef Bones—*Chasen's*
Pasta with Three Cheeses—*Valentino's*
Double Fatburger—*In and Out*
Duck Pizza—*Spago's*
Amaretto Hot Fudge Sundae—*Tonito's*
Chocolate Decadence Cake—*The Ivy*
Tiramisu—*Café Roma*
Apricot Jubilee with Pecan Sauce—*Excelsior*

First I ate myself out of my $15,000 wardrobe. Then I ate so much my picture appeared in the Hollywood *Star* with the caption: EXPECTING?!

One night, Judy Mazel, author of *The Beverly Hills Diet*, saw me at Michel Richard eating a whole frozen chocolate mousse pie—3,500 calories. She said, "Renée, drop your fork and get up from the table quietly and follow me out of here, or I will make a citizen's arrest. Why would you eat that, when only a few weeks ago your figure was perfect?"

"Why?" I said, with a glazed look in my eyes. "Because it was there."

Then I started to get physical symptoms. It was as if I was wrapped in a girdle of pain. Every area of my body hurt but my vagina, which always had a mind of its own. No doctor could understand it. I had pain without weakness. Biopsies were suggested. When the results came back, they said I had amyloids. Joe looked it up in the medical dictionary. It was fatal. We both cried. Joe said he realized how deeply he was connected to me.

The top specialists in Beverly Hills were awestruck that I could function with this amount of pain. That they thought I was "functioning" was a measure of how out of it they were. Anyway, the lab called. It was a mistake—I didn't have amyloids. Someone else's biopsies were mixed up with mine. Then what the hell was causing my symptoms? It's humiliating to tell you the cause. I decided it was what you call "show-business pains," from not being a big enough movie star. I went back to eating to celebrate that I was going to live.

7
DESPERATION DIETING

When I got as fat as I had ever been, size sixteen, Joe ran into the head of another studio in the parking lot of the Hollywood Bowl.

"I happened to read a screenplay that you and Renée wrote, and I'm very interested in doing it with both of you," he said.

(It was a comedy about a diet-pill junkie and an alcoholic rehabilitating each other, called *A Cry for Love*.)

"Great," Joe said. "We're available."

"Give Renée my love," said the studio president. "I just saw her mother at the hot dog stand. She looks exactly like her."

When we got home, Joe told me the story.

"I was too embarrassed to tell him that wasn't your mother, that was you. I love you fat. I love you thin, but they'll never put you in this picture unless you lose 50 pounds."

"How much time do I have to lose it?" I asked.

"Three months."

"I can do it standing on one foot," I bragged.

Quietly, I panicked because I knew that now the bingeing temper tantrum was over, it was going to be twice as hard to take the weight off.

First, I went to a friend of Georgia Brown's who is a famous psychic nutritionist. She told me to clean myself out for two days by eating nothing but avocados. When I looked at the scale after a day and a half I had gained 2 pounds. I went on to the next diet: Dr. Petrie's The Lazy Lady's Easy Diet of 800 calories a day.

Dr. Petrie's The Lazy Lady's Easy Diet

Breakfast: 1 egg, any style
1 piece of melba toast
Coffee or tea
Lunch: 4 ounces of meat or fish
1 cup of salad with diet dressing, or
1 cup of vegetables
1 piece of fruit
Dinner: 5 ounces of meat or fish
Salad (unlimited)
1 cup cooked vegetable

I also signed up for a daily visit to Countess Syd's Passive Exercise Treatment on Rodeo Drive. (You lie on a table and they plug you with wires that rub down and out the "trouble" fat spots on your body.) Needless to say, I was a failure at both "easy" ways out. I had made it doubly hard on myself, because when you gain quickly and you're over thirty, it's twice as hard to take it off. My hairdresser, who was also Jane Fonda's, suggested that I eat what Jane does when she's overweight.

Dr. Bieler's Soup

Boil parsley, zucchini and string beans in water for 3 minutes, then put in blender with cooking water. Serve hot or cold with cayenne pepper.

This diet worked so well for five days that I thought, since I'm on a semifast, why not go on a total fast?

I went to a prominent Beverly Hills hypnotist to have him put me in a trance and get me in a fasting frame of mind. I had to drop a lot of big names to get the appointment. I told him, "I'm under a lot of pressure to lose weight, so I need drastic measures. Please put me in a trance and tell me food is poison, so I won't eat again until I've made my full weight loss."

"I can't do that because I don't believe that," he said pompously. "I believe that you must eat moderately."

"Who the hell cares what you believe? This session is costing me one hundred dollars. For that price I want to hear 'food is rat poison.' *You* pay me one hundred dollars and I'll tell *you* to eat moderately, okay?"

I was hysterical in my desperation, but he had no sense of humor. He called his nurse, who showed me to the door. A few days later I received his bill anyway. I sent it back with a note scribbled all over it. It said, "FOOD IS RAT POISON," ten times.

Then I got a call from a prominent Hollywood astrologer.

"Renée," the friendly voice said at the other end of the phone. "I saw you in a vision this morning. So I called Celebrity Service for your number because I 'saw' you in danger."

"Danger?"

"How much do you weigh?" the astrologer asked.

"One hundred and forty-five," I fibbed.

"You must trim down or your health will suffer. I'd like to do your chart and put you on an astrological diet. I've done every overweight star in Hollywood. When you eat according to your sign, you'll lose. The positions of the planets rule your eating habits." Then he proceeded to name practically every well-known person in Hollywood and tell me how they'd lost.

"How much do you charge?" I asked.

"Twenty dollars a pound. Two hundred dollars in cash down and the rest of the money after you lose your 50 pounds."

"That's fair."

"I'll drop off your Pisces diet tomorrow. Just tell me what time you were born."

"Five minutes to midnight," I said excitedly.

The next morning my diet was delivered by a messenger in return for the $200 cash.

Renée Taylor's Five-Minutes-to-Midnight Pisces Diet

Breakfast: Prune Juice
Yogurt
Snack: Sardines
Whole-wheat toast
Lunch: Yogurt
4 dried apricot halves
Snack: Skim milk
Dinner: Yogurt
½ cup of spinach
Whole-wheat toast

I couldn't believe this lousy diet, but I started it. A day later, the astrologer called.

"How are you doing with your Pisces diet?" he asked.

"I hate it. Do you have a tie-in with a yogurt factory?" I asked facetiously.

"As a matter of fact, I'm presently doing public relations for Harrisberg Milk Products. And if we have a success with you, they'll give you a big rebate on the diet."

"No thanks," I said. I was so relieved that I was being "had," because it meant I could get off this diet now. Very depressed, I went to see a Beverly Hills psychiatrist who specialized in eating disorders. She was a thin, pretty woman who had appeared on many talk shows. She took one look at me and said, "You are sick. You will be well only when you reach your normal weight."

"Do you mean physically or psychologically?"

"Both," she said. "You've got to get away from this town. I'm going to send you to a place I go whenever I have to lose weight for my diet-book tours or television appearances," and she wrote down the name Rejuvenation Retreat, Bahamas.

"What kind of place is this?"

"It's a place for diet sluts like you, who go from one diet to the other promiscuously. But it's not your fault. It's a disease you have. See, the difference between you and me is that I am always thin and you are corpulent thin even at your lowest weight."

"Oh, my God," I moaned. "I never even heard of being corpulent thin. What's the cure?"

"It's drastic, but all the beautiful people of the world have done it: Dietrich, Chaplin, De Gaulle. All of them went there and did the fertilized raw chicken egg and mineral water diet. Not only will you shed fleshiness, you'll come back looking like your own daughter. I myself am fifteen years older than I look," she said.

So with Joe's blessing—"It'll be an experience"—I packed for the Bahamas.

The night before I left I had my "last meal." *All night long.* That's when I learned that every time I was on the threshold of a new diet, Rule One was: The night before, *gain 5 pounds.*

Last-Meal-Before-Diet Binge

Frankfurters
Macaroni and cheese
Jelly beans
After-dinner mints

Then, because I was leaving town for ten days, I "cleaned" everything out of the refrigerator, like a good wife, because I was leaving Joe behind. My attack was something like the Marabunda, those little red killer ants that invade the Brazilian jungle, eating everything in their path—foliage, cattle, even people. My behavior was so inelegant that as dawn came I thanked God for two things: that there was nothing more in the house to eat except for two donuts for the plane ride, and that I was now only 65 pounds overweight.

On the plane to the Bahamas I read the retreat's brochure.

It promised that in ten days I could reverse my weight gain *and* the aging process at the same time, as well as have a spiritual experience from fasting, for $300 a day.

It is true that Joan of Arc fasted whenever she wanted to hear her "voices," and Moses came down from the mountain with the Ten Commandments after a forty-day fast. So maybe something wonderful was waiting for me in the Bahamas. However, the young, sexy doctor in charge down there looked overweight to me.

"You should have seen how I looked before I began to fast," he said with a wink.

After my ten-day fast, the nurse advised me I would feel "centered" and in control of my body. When I returned home, I would continue fasting only once a week. It all sounded easy enough.

Naturally, they would not take me at the retreat if I was pregnant or hypoglycemic, and the doctor tested me for lots of other conditions, winking all the way. Finding me healthy except for my fat, he prescribed a ten-day regimen consisting of a drink made from a fertilized raw chicken egg and water. I had to close my eyes and hold my nose to drink it. To this day, I start to gag whenever I think of that drink. For ten dollars a shot I got injections of procaine, a chemical similar to novocaine that's supposed to make you young. It's from Rumania and was then illegal in the United States. I also got sheep's urine, which they used as an appetite depressant, for five dollars extra a day.

"By the way, all the heads of state and movie stars who come here have had miraculous results, not only in terms of weight loss, youthful skin appearance and brain power, but best of all, their sex drive was incredible," the sexy doctor said, winking again. Suddenly, I realized he wasn't winking. It was a nervous condition.

The ten days of fasting would have been more difficult if I hadn't been so pleasantly surprised to meet many prominent doctors from all over the world waiting on line for the daily fresh seawater whirlpool baths administered by beautiful young nurses. One doctor asked me if I had had any unusual fantasies while I was there.

"Last night I saw a huge pizza pie, heavy on the peppers, and I was in the center of it. My husband was making love to me from inside the mozzarella. Is that unusual?"

"Not at all," he said. "I dreamed that I came naked out of a cake at a party and I ate the whole cake. The women watching were mad at me that I didn't save them any."

I did come back home 10 pounds thinner, and Joe said I looked much younger.

One of the reasons I looked so good had to do with the thrill of being able to endure a crazy treatment like that. I was so happy with my 10-pound weight loss that I went back to the psychiatrist who had sent me to the Bahamas. Maybe she had another tip for weight loss. Sitting in the waiting room I told one of the male patients there how great she was for helping me. He said, "I'm having an affair with her as part of the treatment."

"I don't believe you. Doctors are not supposed to do that."

"She's very unorthodox. First we fast in the Bahamas to rid our bodies of toxic poisons, then we go to her group and share our fantasies, and then we all have sex. It's very spiritual once you get into it. It's a combination of Indian religion and diet control."

"Are you serious?" I asked incredulously.

"Didn't you ever hear of 'screwing' your way to heaven?" he said, pointing to the pictures on the wall of her waiting room. I hadn't noticed them before. Now, looking closely, I saw they were very erotic paintings of orgies. I was halfway out the door when the doctor came into the outer room and greeted me.

"Renée, you look great. Come in."

I pretended I was only leaving to put money in the meter for my car, because I didn't want to find out if what the man said was the truth. However, she brought it up herself.

"I'd like you to take the next step for weight control and enlightenment."

"You don't mean group sex? I'm very happily married."

"Don't knock what you haven't tried. You and Joe will be happier for the experience. It's not depraved at all. Don't judge these people. My group is not your typical Hollywood group. They are responsible people, pure in heart, like children playing in a sandpile. They are mostly beautiful movie stars, but first, they are people who need to change their body image to feel free of society's repression, and second, they are all committed to helping everyone lose their CT—corpulent thinness," she said.

"Could I go and just watch to see what it's like and keep my clothes on?" I asked, hoping she'd say no.

"I'll have to ask my group. I'll call you and let you know."

I was too ashamed to tell Joe about the conversation. I was just going to forget the whole thing when she called.

"My group said you can come tonight. Eight o'clock at my house."

All I could think about was, what if I run into someone I know? I don't want to see them naked and/or having sex. But I felt I had to see for myself what people were doing in the name of religion and body transformation. And also, I'd pick up a few weight-loss tips. Naturally, I had no intention of telling Joe.

I changed clothes a dozen times. Finally I decided to wear a bathing suit under my dress, which I would take off when I got there so I wouldn't stand out too much.

My heart was beating very fast as I entered the house. The doctor, who was naked, was lecturing two fat young girls on burning calories. She took me around the house and introduced me to everyone by first names only. We were all supposed to pretend we didn't know anyone there. I only knew of them. I was very embarrassed to see them there, and I was careful to look only in their eyes and not at their genitalia. At least half of the group was recognizable from the movie colony—actors, writers, producers and directors. When I said I was only an "observer," they all laughed and said they were "observers" the first time too. I tried to act very casual, noticing people making love in the hot tub and under a papier-mâché waterfall in the pool. I walked into the library. People wearing towels were sitting on chairs, waiting for a movie to begin. Without thinking, I sat down, not knowing what else to do. The film began. It was the most explicit hard-core porno movie I had ever seen.

"Excuse me, I saw this movie already," I said as I left the room.

I opened another door. It was a sauna, and people were making love right there on the wood slats. A woman caught my eye.

"He's reaching his climax," she told me.

"Thank you for sharing that," I said and closed the door.

Finally, with no place to go without people having sex, I walked over to the food table, joining a woman who was about 10 pounds overweight.

"Have you ever been to Hugh Hefner's mansion?" she asked me softly.

"No."

"Well, don't say I said, but his buffet is much more nutritious, and he's not even into weight loss."

A few days later, I got up the courage to tell Joe I had gone to the weight-loss orgy.

"Boy, are you brave," he said. "I could never go. Promise me one thing. If you ever hear of any of my childhood idols, like Cary Grant, going to her orgy, please don't tell me."

(I never did hear that, and I wouldn't have told him even if I had.)

Time was running out for me get to my shooting weight. There were sixty-five days to go, and I still had 50 pounds to lose. I bumped into Lanie Kazan, who told me she was on the Last Chance Diet and losing 1 pound a day. It was truly my last chance. My secretary, Ruth Horne, and I went on it together.

Last Chance Diet

Breakfast: 2 ounces Proline
Lunch: 2 ounces Proline
Dinner: 2 ounces Proline
Snack: 2 ounces Proline

I began to lose a pound a day, and even though I had some side effects—gas and hair falling out—I was on a high. Ruth was not so lucky. She wasn't losing. The doctor who put us on the diet told her she must be cheating. Well, Joe and I knew she wasn't. She was spending a hundred dollars a week at his office and not losing, and she couldn't afford it. So Joe and I both went with her on the next visit and told the doctor we were witnesses to her only drinking her protein "fix." From then on he didn't charge Ruth unless she lost. It turned out she had hypoglycemia, and that's why the Last Chance Diet took twice as long for her. I was lucky. I lost 40 pounds in sixty-five days.

Then something happened that only happens in Hollywood. Just as we were ready to make *A Cry for Love,* the president of the studio was fired and a new president was installed. He loved Joe for the alcoholic, but for my role of the diet junkie he wanted a superstar whom I had met and admired. I was immobilized. I couldn't tell Joe *not* to do it without me, nor could I tell him to go ahead and do it without me. I was so catatonic I couldn't even speak. In thinking about doing the new movie, we borrowed money in advance from a bank and bought our first house in Beverly Hills. It was a huge English Tudor with a rose garden in front and a goldfish pond on the side and a swimming pool in a jungle in the back. It had been Shirley Temple's honeymoon house when she married John Agar. There's a large strawberry patch in the back near the swimming pool. When I met her at a luncheon, she laughingly told me she was a peanut-butter addict. In those days, the studio weighed their stars every morning. And whenever she overdid it she'd eat nothing but strawberries for a whole day to lose the extra pounds before anyone at the studio noticed her weight gain.

"Whatever you decide, Renée, it's okay with me," Joe said to me.

"No, Joe. Whatever you decide is okay with me."

To my surprise, Joe refused to do the movie without me, even though we needed the money. I was just 20 pounds away from my movie weight, but I felt so guilty that he didn't do the film without me that I went "unconscious" in my eating habits. A friend of mine got me an audience with her guru, Baba Muktananda, thinking he could stop me from blaming myself for Joe's sacrifice. After I told Baba the story, he told me, "Chant," and he gave me an Indian name, *Lolakamanlalli*, which means Lover of Lotus Flowers. I kneeled and kissed his feet, and he put a chocolate in my mouth. Then he hit me on the head with a long white feather. Out in the hall, I asked my friend what each part of the ceremony meant.

"Baba was telling you with your Indian name that Joe is the male lotus flower you were born to love. With the chocolate in your mouth he was telling you that life is not all dieting. You must eat sweets too. Baba was telling you with the feather hit that you now have *shakti*, which means he has given you magic to shake you out of your depression."

I was so happy to hear all the good news that I chanted for days. The chocolate part pleased me too. A holy man had told me to forget about dieting. I was off on a new toot. I could eat chocolate whenever I wanted. I found it curbed my appetite between meals, but it kept me stout. Once, around two o'clock in the morning, I was scrounging in the freezer for chocolate Christmas cookies, but Joe had already been there at 1:00 A.M.

Joe had gotten as fat as me, I guess to show his loyalty. If he got a call for a movie, he'd say he didn't want to be in it unless I was in it too. It was like the theme of *The Flying Dutchman*—the measure of a lover's devotion is how much he is willing to give up for you. Or it was also like being in the O. Henry story

"The Gift of the Magi," where a man sells his watch to buy a comb for a woman, and she sells her hair to buy him a watch fob. Ultimately, their only possession is their love for each other.

Joe and I were headed in that direction. Our friend and accountant, Marty Melzer, warned us we were getting deeper and deeper in debt. Marty told another friend of ours about our financial woes. He wasn't a rich man, but Barry Wolf lent us enough money to live on for three years. We had never worried before, but now we started worrying about how we would ever pay Barry back. (We finally did this year!)

Then we both had a great idea at the same time. Since we couldn't afford to live in our Beverly Hills house anymore and we hated the idea of selling it, why not rent it out for a lot of money, live someplace cheaper and write a play—a two-character play that we'd both star in. On Broadway, the playwright has the final say on casting, so we'd be together again writing and acting. "But, we have to pick a place to write in that forces us to have a peak experience," I said.

"Vermont!" said Joe. "It's impossible not to write deeply in Vermont."

So we packed up the Beverly Hills house and moved with our son, Gabriel, to Barnard, Vermont. We rented a cute little farmhouse and had a real Vermont experience.

I went on the Scarsdale International Diet.

Scarsdale International Diet

Monday—American Day: Barbecued steak
Tuesday—Japanese Day: Shrimp and chicken
Wednesday—French Day: Tarragon chicken
Thursday—Italian Day: Veal napoletana
Friday—Spanish Day: Gazpacho
Saturday—Greek Day: Lamb with Dolmas
Sunday—Hawaiian Day: Pineapple Surprise Aloha

I lost weight, but as soon as I went off the diet I gained again. Later on I felt sympathy for Jean Harris. She should have put Dr. Tarnower in a room and made him go on his own diet. That would have been punishment enough.

Joe's health had suffered from his large weight gain, and the fat level in his blood was up. We heard that the Pritikin diet helped reduce serum cholesterol, so we both went on it for three months.

The Pritikin Quick Weight Loss Diet

Breakfast: 3.5 ounces cooked oatmeal (plus bran)
4 ounces non-fat milk
½ orange

Lunch: 8 ounces chili pepper soup
4 ounces raw bell pepper
4 ounces raw carrots
4 ounces raw cauliflower
4 ounces raw cucumbers

Dinner: 8 ounces tomato rice soup
8 ounces shredded cabbage, onions and tomatoes
8 ounces stuffed eggplant

I bought the Pritikin recipe book, and because there was a large dairy down the road, I started making cheese and baking bread from the recipes. We ran 3 miles every day to the general store, and I learned to cross-country ski. The writing was very hard. We had no idea a two-character play would be so difficult to write or we never would have attempted it. But it was like a second honeymoon for us, living so simply in Barnard. Our best friends from Beverly Hills, Jerry and Beverly Kramer, came to visit and were very envious of how idyllic and unostentatious our life was. When spring came, we picked wildflowers, and it looked like we would never finish our play. After six months we were still on our first act.

Gabriel began having trouble keeping up in school because he had a slight learning disability. They wanted to put him back one grade to give him an easier time, but Joe and I weren't sure that was the best thing for him. Just then, the president of a network called and asked us to sell *A Cry for Love* to them for two big television stars. We decided to be practical, take the money, and go back home to Beverly Hills. We now had to take the rich people who had rented our house to court for the rent they never had paid. We put Gabriel in school in Beverly Hills, and, with help, his work caught up and he seemed much happier.

Suddenly, I was called by two different networks to do a television series. In one I had to be thin. In the other, I had to be nine-months pregnant. I chose to make the pilot where I was thin first, and I went to the Rancho La Puerta spa in Mexico to lose weight. I lost 7 pounds in ten days. Joe came on the weekend and lost 5 pounds.

Rancho La Puerta Diet

Breakfast: Grapefruit, papaya or orange
Hot 7-grain cereal
Coffee, herb tea or decaffeinated coffee
Lunch: Acidophilus (yogurt culture drink)
Barley soup
Vegetable salad with yogurt dressing
Fresh fruit
Dinner: Minestrone soup
Mexican salad—jicama and oranges with lettuce
Zucchini lasagna with mushrooms and broccoli
Vanilla flan (like custard)

The president of the network loved the pilot. I was being signed to a million-dollar deal. Joe and I and Gabriel went to Tahiti to celebrate with an extravagant vacation.

I was so happy in Bora Bora—it was paradise. The people there seemed to laugh at everything and anything. At first, I thought they were crazy. Then I realized I was the crazy one. I soon found out that when you're in paradise and you're dining on mangoes and mahi-mahi fish, what's not to laugh at? Joe and Gabriel and I found an awesomely beautiful spot half in the water, half under a tree that we called our "laughing place." Once a day we would go there and hold each other, making a people sandwich and giggling from joy. Floating in the lagoon, I let go of all my struggles. I absolved everyone who could ever hurt me. It was such a liberating experience to have no resentments. I couldn't tell where I ended and the water and the sky began. I was one with the universe. If I died right there it would have been okay, because I would have continued as part of this Divine Beauty.

When we were ready to come back, our lawyer told us that in the middle of his negotiations with the network, the president who hired me was fired and had left for Bora Bora. I met him in Tahiti at the airport. As we were leaving, he was arriving. He looked as if he was having a breakdown. I tried to console him by showing him my new collection of seashells. I picked out a Golden Cone and gave it to him as a present. "Try to feel One with the Universe," I told him.

Now I felt I had to make the pregnant-woman show in a hurry before something happened to the other television president. My friend Bob Goldfarb, a vice-president at the network, warned me his superiors were reading the want ads. I was very anxious and started eating for two. Pretty soon, I was convinced that I was pregnant again. My gynecologist told me it was just "common, garden-variety fat."

One morning, I was out picking up the newspaper in front of the house in my robe, and just as I was bending down, a bus load of tourists stopped in front of the house. A woman yelled to her husband, "Quick, Harold, get a picture of that lady's rear end. I want our friends in Philly to see a picture of someone who's ten times as fat as me and lives in Beverly Hills." I knew it was time to try something drastic for weight loss again. It was summer. Gabriel was at camp in the East and we still hadn't finished our play.

I saw an ad in *Prevention* magazine for a "fast farm" in Lew Beach, New York, called Rose's Health Juice Fasting Spa—forty dollars a day for two people.

"Let's sign up," I said. "We'll finish our play and fast together for the same price."

"I could never skip *one* meal without getting a headache," Joe said to me. "How could I go for a week?"

"If a fat woman can do it, so can a big man. Anyway, don't you want to be thin before we get to Broadway?"

I'm sure that thought helped him to be a good sport and try the fast with me. Rose's place was a big farmhouse in an apple orchard. She ran a very friendly and informal spa, but she took the juice fasting very seriously. She told us we could have light meals if we wanted, but once we chose the juice fast, we couldn't switch, as it would be a bad example to her other guests. Joe and I committed ourselves to only fresh apple juice and water five times a day. Then the fun began.

The first day was rough. We were starving and we sunned ourselves and slept a lot, or maybe we passed out from feeling dumb at committing ourselves to just apple juice and water. Then it got rougher. By the end of the second day, Joe was making my life a living hell for bringing him there. All he talked about was great Italian meals he'd had. Soon, I was obsessed about food too. I had new food fantasies about white bread with mayonnaise and American cheese—things I had never eaten. Then I told Joe about an Italian restaurant I once went to in Scranton, Pennsylvania, called Mario's, where they served the best veal chop calabrese, a huge veal chop with hot peppers, and home fries.

"Let's go have some," he said.

"Never. I am staying on apple juice just to prove that my body is a temple to be worshipped."

I had read that somewhere and I guess the idea appealed to Joe, so he hung in on the fast. After all, our skin was getting rosy, and he had lost 4 pounds. Me, only 1½. Men have more water in their bodies than women, so they lose quicker.

Then after five days, he'd lost 10 pounds. I'd lost 3. Only two more days to go. We were irritable but we were writing well, and in my spare moments I browsed through Rose's library filled with books on the lives of famous fasters and their body results. I read about Arnold Schultz, a fat man who fasted and cured his crippling arthritis and obesity. He claimed that papaya juice brought him emotional stability, and he swore that he had also *reversed* the aging process. He looked younger at fifty-eight than he did at thirty-five. I studied his before and after photos and I agreed with him. Then I turned to the last pages and read the editor's note. After twenty-three years of juice fasting, Arnold Schultz was run over by a truck. At the time of his death, he never looked better.

All of a sudden, I wanted to live and eat as I never had before. A few minutes after our dinner of apple juice and water, Joe and I sneaked out of Rose's place and drove for two and a half hours to Mario's Restaurant in Scranton, Pennsylvania, and had the veal chop calabrese. I blew my five-day fasting on a great greasy dinner, but it was a good lesson.

The biggest disadvantage to fasting is that if you go back to bingeing, you put the weight back on twice as fast because you have screwed up your metabolism. Joe felt lucky just to have discovered that he could go five days without solid food, and I found myself a partner in juice fasting around the country for the summer.

Next, I took Joe with me to Anne Wigmore's Hippocratic Health Center in Boston. Anne is seventy years old and has written many books on the healing powers of wheatgrass. When a sick cow grazes on wheatgrass, it's cured overnight. I was anxious to see what it could do for me too. Anne does her own sprouting at her institute, and you can eat three vegetarian meals a day or just juices. This time, Joe did the sprouts and vegetable juice regimen and I fasted, eating only wheatgrass. I also took it internally by squeezing the contents of a small round bag of wheatgrass juice up my rectum, twice a day, after giving myself a high-colonic enema. It sounds bizarre and it is, but it makes you look and feel great because you rid yourself of toxic poisons. A friend of mine who tried this internal method had both of her legs turn green until her body discharged the juice—that's how filled with poison she was.

Anne says she cured herself of all kinds of serious illnesses when she was a young girl, including saving her leg, which the doctors wanted to amputate because she had gangrene. She watched a sick baby lamb cure itself by eating wheatgrass, that's how she discovered her cure. Anne only sleeps four hours a night, yet she has boundless energy from the grass. She walks 5 miles a day and looks fabulous. That is, she looks fabulous if she *is* seventy. If she is any younger than that, it's definitely *aging* her looks!

There's only one down side of squirting wheatgrass up inside you. Who would want to do it indefinitely, no matter how healthy you feel or how thin you are? I lost 7 pounds in ten days, but it was a pretty boring procedure and a real pain in the rear, pun intended. I was also tempted to try it because Anne said continual use of wheatgrass postpones menopause, but Anne also says she can still have a baby at seventy. Unfortunately, she can't prove it because she also believes in celibacy.

Anne is a doctor, however, and winner of the Nobel Peace Prize for bringing sprouts to Third World countries to combat hunger. All of her patients claim health improvements, but they are committed to her program as a permanent lifestyle. She helped me set up a wheatgrass farm in my house in Beverly Hills the following year. I tried it for a few months, but slowly my old bad habits crept into my life. Last year she came to visit to see how I was doing, but she saw a can of Diet Coke sitting on my kitchen table. She backed away and out the door as if I had betrayed her, nutritionally, and I never heard from her again.

I still believe in wheatgrass for deep cleansing, and for feeding the underprivileged and sick. And if, God forbid, I ever get some awful disease, I know I will turn to it again, although not for weight loss. Joe says he would not ever cleanse himself that way for anything, but he enjoyed drinking the sprout juice for a quick loss of 14 pounds in ten days, and he would do it again if he were ever desperate.

The last place we fasted together was the New Age Health Farm in Neva Sink, New York. A weekend fast there is good for 3½ pounds for me and 5 to 7 pounds for Joe. It's a very strict place where you may only have a variety of fruit juices during the day and vegetable broth for dinner. The manager scolded me for putting too much parsley on top of my broth.

"Miss Taylor, the parsley is not to be used as a food. Only as a garnish," she said, grabbing the handful I had stolen from the kitchen off my soup plate.

We finished writing our Broadway play, *It Had To Be You*, at this spartan place, hungry but proud of ourselves. By the way, if you're unmarried and a woman, juice fasting is a very quick way to make men friends. Men are more open to a relationship when they are hungry, and they need more hugging then too!

8

BROADWAY LULLABY, HOLLYWOOD SONATA

It was 1981, and I couldn't imagine anything more exciting than opening on Broadway in my own two-character comedy with the man I loved. The producer, Allen Klein, suggested I go to the Golden Door in San Diego to lose 10 more pounds before I had my first costume fitting.

"It costs $3,000 a week, who can afford it?" I asked.

"I'm treating my star," he said. (I couldn't believe he meant me!)

All I can say about "The Door" is that it's worth every penny, if you can find an angel to send you. I lost 8 pounds in a pampered week.

Golden Door Diet

Breakfast: 1 plain poached egg
½ piece of Golden Door bread
Coffee or tea with cream and sugar

Lunch: Grilled chicken salad with fresh garden tomatoes and sprouts
Chilled papaya-orange soup

Dinner: Japanese miso soup with tofu and chives
Barbecued shrimp kabob with grilled pineapple
Fried rice

(The balance of calories—to a total of 900—is made up with juices and other introduced snacks: 10:00 A.M. break—potassium broth, 6:30 P.M. cocktail hour—stuffed mushrooms, sushi rolls.)

When Joe and I arrived in New York, Allen had extravagantly arranged for our photos to be taken by Scavullo, the best glamour photographer in New York, for $10,000. On his walls were pictures he had taken of Sophia, Liz, Rita, even Garbo. I was made up and coiffed for two hours before the session began. I kept thinking how this photo was something I would treasure my whole life, no matter what happened to the play. When I walked out on the white paper I was to be photographed on, my knees were shaking. "So what kind of a picture did you have in mind?" Scavullo asked me in a thick foreign accent.

"Huh? I thought maybe you would have some ideas." I wanted to add "at these prices," but I didn't dare.

He stared at me for a long time. "I'm looking at you, but I'm not getting anything."

"You're not? . . . How's this?" I said, feeling like a failure, and I proceeded to imitate the poses of all the great movie stars on his walls, plus the ones I remembered from my childhood of Rita and Betty and Lana, and Garbo, with her face cupped in her hands.

My Garbo imitation pose was blown up and used over the entrance to the theater. The Golden Theater on West Forty-fifth Street was a real prize. It was the one everyone wanted. We got it from the Shuberts by reading the play for them in the living room of our first producers, Isobel Robbins and her husband, Ron Konecky. Before we began I said, "If you don't like this one, we have another one."

"I hope your play is as funny as you are," one of the Shuberts said.

When we finished reading, the other Shubert said, "We'll give you our Golden Theater. I haven't laughed this much since my brother died."

"I hope you're going to lose weight before you open," the first Shubert said.

"I'd like to see her put on 10 pounds," said the other.

This was definitely a double messsage. Whenever I saw them after that I would tell one I was gaining, the other I was losing.

"Give me your diet for my wife," one of them asked during a rehearsal at the theater, but I couldn't remember whether he was the one who told me to lose or the one who told me to gain, so I just said, "I'm on Polly Bergen's diet. I have dessert every other day, but I only eat half of it. It's called having your cake and eating it too."

Polly Bergen's Diet

Breakfast: 2 scrambled eggs
2 pieces of crisp toast
Lunch: Cold cuts
Cheese or cottage cheese
English muffin or piece of toast
Pickles or olives
Dinner: Steak
Salad

That's when it hit me what a good idea it would be to eat that way—to control my binges. And I began storing up information that I would eventually use on my Taylor-Made Diet.

Mel Brooks stopped by the theater one day to say hello. I worked for him in *The Producers*. I played Eva Braun to Dick Shawn's Hitler. "You look good," I said. "What diet are you on?"

Slipping immediately into the character of the two-thousand-year-old man, he said, "Why should I diet? I never eat. I don't even know why I'm fat. I don't eat anything. Maybe some orange juice for breakfast, that's all. Okay, a piece of toast this big, but it's rye, or sometimes one egg. Simple, scrambled, a little piece of bacon, you can hardly see it. A few potatoes, boiled only, a sprig of parsley, that's all! Maybe a prune danish, no butter, and some raisins and a few nuts and that's it. Nothing in my mouth all day except maybe lunch. I have a little fish, with a vegetable, a hard roll, some applesauce, dietetic; coffee, skim milk, ices, maybe with a little fresh pineapple on top. A cookie, to kill the aftertaste; and nothing between meals, except maybe a box of Goobers, a few M&Ms, a bite of pizza maybe, for taste, and that's it until dinner when I eat nothing. Absolutely zilch except if I'm hungry, a shrimp cocktail, a few hors d'oeuvres on a cracker; a cube of cheese so small a dog would refuse it; a plain salad, no dressing; a spoonful of spaghetti, no meatballs; a thin slice of veal, a smidge of Parmesan or you can't eat it; a drop of minestrone to push everything down; maybe a drop of Jell-O with make-believe whipped cream on top; a few after-dinner mints and that's it for the whole day, except maybe for a piece of chicken and a glass of wine in the middle of the night if I can't sleep, usually from worry that I'm fat and I don't know why."

We had a good laugh, and whenever I binged after that I would think of how little I ate too.

Then a strange thing happened. I had trouble remembering my lines, so I went to a hypnotist.

"I don't understand it. I wrote my lines myself. It took me over three and a half years and now I can't remember them."

"It's only stress," the hypnotist said. "Your whole identity is wrapped up in this play."

He hypnotized me so that I could imagine myself in a huge bubble flying over an audience of all the great people who had ever lived: Jesus, Joan of Arc, Moses, etc. This imagination exercise calmed me down and helped me to remember my lines. I couldn't figure out why Joe wasn't as nervous as I was, and then I realized that the "theater" meant more to me because I had been an actress for twenty years. For me, starring on Broadway was realizing a dream, while Joe was just getting one.

Opening night, Mike Nichols sent us a good-luck telegram that I taped to my mirror: "I hope you have a great big HAT," he said.

After a standing ovation from the audience, our friends Bella and Martin Abzug, Elaine May, Chuck Grodin, Marlo Thomas, Beverly and Jerry Kramer, and Rita and Morrie Pynos came backstage with buckets of caviar to congratulate us.

In front of everyone, my brother Bernard, who was out of work, said, "I don't want to wait for the reviews to ask you if I can borrow $500." Bobby Drivas, the brilliant director of the play, and Julian Schlossberg, the co-producer, both told him, "Ask for a thousand." I laughed and wrote out a check.

I couldn't have been happier with the audience's reaction on opening night. They laughed continuously for two hours during *It Had to Be You*. Marlo Thomas, who was instrumental in getting the play done on Broadway, had taken us out for a champagne dinner the night before, to celebrate. "You'll run forever," she said, toasting us. In a way we have. The play went on to be a hit in Los Angeles, Israel, Greece, Japan, Denmark and even China. As we go to press, it's been playing in Paris for a year. However, on Broadway we ran only three months, as long as *Lovers and Other Strangers*.

The reviews for Joe and me were raves, all except one important reviewer who obviously didn't "get" me or the play. The story tells about a desperate actress who auditions for a commercial by bringing the producer home to her apartment. Like Scheherazade, she entertains him for twenty-four hours, and they run the whole gamut of emotions together. The next morning he realizes that he needs her in his life, he proposes marriage, and they decide to write and be successful together. The one negative reviewer said I played too "vulnerably" and I was *miscast* in the part. I had written it for myself about myself, yet this guy said I wasn't right for the part.

Even though that seems funny to me now, I went into shock then. I was totally unprepared not to have a huge popular success. It was the worst thing that had ever happened to me. It reminded me of the time my mother said, "Go show the neighbors how pretty you look," and they slammed the door in my face. We had spent almost three years writing the play. I thought because our intention was pure—to share our insights about relationships between men and women—the play would have tremendous acceptance. I was even more devastated because, ironically, I was counting on getting the recognition as an actress that I didn't get for *Lovers and Other Strangers*.

Of course, I will go back to Broadway again and again and take my chances. Why? Because that's what I do. I write and I act; which reminds me of a favorite joke of mine. An emcee announces, "Now, Madame X will sing for you . . ." From the audience someone yells out, "She's a whore." The emcee says, "Nevertheless, she will now sing *La Bohème*."

What I learned from the *It Had to Be You* closing was that I could let go of the hope but not the dream, when something didn't come out the way I wanted. It was the first time in my life I said, *"Thy* will be done." It was all too much for me to understand. So I put it in the hands of our Creator.

While Joe and I were writing *Lovers and Other Strangers*, Elaine May recommended us to doctor a show that was floundering out of town. When we started working, people were walking out in droves. One night, we watched the show with some of our writing in it from the back of the house. We were so excited at the response from the audience. We jumped up and down. We ran to the phone to call Elaine to tell her of our success. "We've gotten the walkouts down to only ten people," we told her proudly. We had taken the job with the provision that we could keep our names off the credits, because we didn't want to be responsible for what we didn't write.

When the play opened on Broadway, someone leaked to the critics that we had rewritten the show. The reviewer said, "We heard Renée Taylor and Joseph Bologna really wrote this show and that they are married. It's a good thing that they have each other. That's all they have." Joe and I were spending Christmas in Vermont when that show opened. We drove to a general store to buy the New York newspapers. I read the review out loud to Joe. We hugged each other and cried for a long time because of what the reviewer said about us. It was snowing very hard outside the car window. Joe finally said quietly, "If that's all we do have, I'll settle for that."

When *It Had to Be You* ended its run, I started to discover that my most important creation was my life with Joe and Gabriel. That kept me from having a total nervous breakdown. One night before we closed I got a call in my dressing room.

"Hello, this is Burt Reynolds."

"Oh, sure, and I'm Lana Turner," I said. "Say something in 'Burt Reynolds.'"

"I love you."

"Hello, Burt!"

"How'd you and Joe like to bring your play to my place in Florida? And write a screenplay for me at the same time."

"Are you kidding? We'd love it."

"Burt's Florida theater," I yelled to Joe. "I'm going to get even thinner."

When the play closed on Broadway, I was on the Champagne Diet from *Vogue* magazine.

Champagne Diet

Breakfast: ½ cup orange juice
1 egg, scrambled in double boiler
1 slice whole-wheat toast
1 glass of champagne

Lunch: Mixed green salad
1 slice cold salmon
1 bran muffin
½ cantaloupe
1 glass of champagne

Dinner: Filet of beef
Carrots, cooked
⅔ cup strawberries
1 glass of champagne

I was losing 3 pounds a week and was well on my way to becoming a drunk. I never had a drinking problem before, but now I was hooked on the champagne. After one week I couldn't have just one glass of champagne and "too much wasn't enough," as the saying goes. A few months later I found out I was allergic to grapes and that's why I became addicted to champagne, but then I didn't know it. A nutritionist friend of mine advised me that Dom Pérignon and Cristal had fewer calories than cheaper champagne, so now my "habit" was costing $100 a day.

All through our run at Burt's theater I was on a champagne high. No one seemed to notice except Joe. When he commented on it, I said, "It's helping me lose weight." And it was, since I was eating less. All I cared about was my "fix" at the end of the meal. I pointed out how much all the critics had liked me here in Florida. "Maybe my drinking champagne had something to do with our being nominated for 'Best Play of the Season.' Haven't I been wittier since I've been on this diet, and more imaginative while we were writing our screenplay for Burt too?"

These were all typical "insights" of the alcoholic I had become, as I found out later in Rio.

Shortly after we closed in Florida, Joe was making a movie in Rio, and I visited him twice. He was lonely and he wanted me to come very much. I was still writing the first draft of Burt's screenplay, and I was happy to go back and forth on the long plane trip to Brazil, particularly because they were pouring French champagne for the whole trip.

The first night there Michael Caine and his wife, Shakira, invited us out to an elegant nightclub. I must have been tipsy when I arrived at the club, because when a strange man sat down next to me and asked me to get him an interview with

Michael Caine, I said, "Sure. For a bottle of Dom Pérignon."

I never would have done that sober. A bottle was sent to our table and I proceeded to polish it off. Michael and his wife were dancing when Joe and I said goodbye and thanked them for a lovely evening.

Outside on the street, Joe was hailing a cab as I tripped and landed facedown in the gutter. I must have passed out for a few minutes, because the next thing I knew Joe and I were in a taxi and Joe was crying.

"Seeing you lying there in the gutter, after you made a complete fool of yourself with Michael and Shakira, promising an interview for a bottle of champagne, I realized how much I love you," he said.

"Who, me? A fool of myself? I thought I was cute tonight."

I really did think that. Passing out was cute. That thought kept going over and over in my mind. Was it cute or was it inappropriate behavior? No, it was very appropriate if I was a wino. Joe knew I had become a wino, and look how he loved me.

My son Gabriel was starting Beverly Hills High. The first day he came home and said, "I like poor kids better. They have a lot of drug and alcohol problems. At least their parents go to AA at the school at night. Why don't you go too, Ma? You act silly when you drink one glass of champagne."

That's all I needed to hear. I was out the door on my way to my first AA meeting. Naturally, I loved going. I told them all about how close I had come to disaster in my marriage and my career. Then I met Dr. Stuart Berger, and I went on his Immune Power Diet for six months and started to feel really great because I cut out the forty-five foods I am allergic to.

Dr. Berger's Immune Power Diet

Breakfast: ½ cup strawberries
½ cup oatmeal
1 cup fresh, unsweetened orange juice
Coffee substitute or herbal tea

Lunch: 4 ounces broiled chicken
1 cup steamed green beans
1 cup steamed potatoes
1 kiwi
Mineral water or seltzer
Dinner: Parsnip and leek soup
4 ounces broiled chicken
1 cup sautéed okra or steamed green beans
Swiss chard or endive salad (unlimited)
Citrus salad dressing
½ cup strawberries
Coffee substitute, herbal tea

Dr. Berger's diet taught me that there were foods that I was both allergic and addicted to, and if I ate any of them they triggered a binge. The bad news was that for the most part they were things that I loved, like tuna fish. I was surprised to find that I was allergic to lettuce, celery, wheat and asparagus, but that's because I had eaten so much of them during my lifetime.

Then there were coffee, flour, eggs and sugar, which meant coffee cake was out. So I started experimenting with what I *could* eat. If I am allergic to wheat, what would happen if I had artichoke and spinach pasta all day, since one food at a time is easier to digest?

For one day I ate nothing but pasta, and lost a pound! For the first time, I started to think about a diet of one food a day, as if my food for the week were a seven-course meal. Eventually, that formula led to my Taylor-Made Diet.

Then Bella Abzug and I went to see Shirley MacLaine perform at a benefit. Backstage, she introduced me to a man named Jach who was a "channel" for a Being called Lazaris. I wasn't sure what that meant until Bella explained that Lazaris was an "energy" without a body, as old as the beginning of the world. He was a Celestial Being who came to visit a human woman named Peny, Jach's wife, who had lived many times before now. Lazaris loved her because she was an unusually caring, fun-loving, insightful person whom he wanted to be with. She persuaded him to stay and meet the rest of us mortals and teach us the secrets of the universe. I thought it was outrageously farfetched, but I went to see Jach in San Francisco anyway because Beverly Dennis, my psychiatrist friend, had heard his tapes on "Manifesting Your Reality," and asked me to go with her. During a meditation session, Lazaris called my name out in a darkened room of 200 people.

"Renée, surrender to your diet. You needn't struggle with it. It's fun. Don't make things so hard."

I couldn't understand how he could know that about me. A few weeks later in a private session, with Lazaris coming to me through Jach, I said, "I hate to bother you with something as insignificant as my diet, when you've come to earth to be our Spiritual Guide. Could you enlighten me as to what I'm supposed to be doing with my food, instead of struggling with it?"

"Close your eyes. See yourself in a dark pine forest. Do you see a fat little girl who was you at six? I want you to hold her in your arms and forgive her fat," Lazaris said.

"Forgive her fat?"

"Yes. She's hurting because she feels you've judged her fatness and she's holding onto it until you forgive it."

"I didn't mean to judge it," I answered.

"Have you hated her fat?"

"Yes, I have," I admitted.

"Then you've judged it. Forgive her fat and tell her you want her to surrender, and she'll play getting thin and staying thin with you."

I held the fat little girl in my arms and I kissed her eyes and my tears dripped on her cheeks and, together, we cried for a long time. Then we took a walk in the forest with a deer, which Lazaris told me was the animal I was before I was born a person. We were then joined by me as an even younger, but thinner, child of three years old.

"What if we had a party and ate a different course of a banquet every day of the week? Would that be fun for you?" I asked my fat little girl.

"Oh, yes," she answered.

We all joined hands in a circle and danced and laughed until we dropped—the fat little girl, my thin little girl, my deer and me. One by one, other animals came and watched us, followed by the Mother of us all and her Mother.

I told my fat friend next door about my experience with Lazaris, hoping it would help her too. She had gained 100 pounds in six weeks. How can anyone gain 100 pounds in six weeks? By practicing. One day, she was so excited when I told her on the phone that I was baking cookies that she crashed her car in her hurry to get to my house to try them. I visited her in the hospital with the cookies. I baked them with fruit juice and egg whites and soy beans, because we were both allergic to sugar, flour and yolks.

It was ten o'clock in the morning, and I couldn't believe what she was doing. She had an IV in her arm and she was stuffing herself with pizza that had just been delivered from Numero Uno.

"Are you crazy? You're killing yourself!"

"I don't know why I do it," she said, crying while she ate the pizza.

"If you want to know *why* you overeat, stop doing it."

"I'm hungry."

"You can't eat until you're full—you'll never be full. You have to eat until you decide you're through eating," I said, crying too. I knew I was finding out things about myself as I confronted her. The only difference between her and me was that she was 100 pounds heavier.

Then Joe got a part in a mini-series called *Sins*, with Joan Collins and Lauren Hutton, to be filmed in Paris, Nice and Venice. He begged me to come with him. With two beautiful women playing his wife and his mistress, he said, "I'm scared . . . I'll overeat." I went with him and helped him with his diet as I continued to study mine. It was hard not to overdose with French food. This is the diet Joan Collins went on:

Joan Collins' Le Régime Parisien

- *Breakfast:* Fraises des bois
  Café au lait
- *Lunch:* Navarin of lamb
  Salade pissenlit
  Brie
  Beaujolais
- *Dinner:* Truite au bleu
  Pommes anglaise
  Pyramide (chèvre)
  Fraises des bois
  Saint-Émilion

Lauren Hutton had her own variation:

Lauren Hutton's Five-Day Melt Away Wine Diet

- *Breakfast:* Sliced bananas with cream
  Tea with lemon
  Côtes du Rhône, white and red
- *Lunch:* Asparagus
  Baked endive
  Baked ham
  Tomato salad, goat cheese
  1 slice of bread
  Anjou rosé
- *Dinner:* Cold shrimp
  Cheese soufflé
  Mushroom salad
  Pineapple with kirsch
  Muscadet
  Black coffee

I couldn't go on either of these diets because they included wine. Besides, I knew they weren't right for me. I had to find a life plan for eating that I could enjoy.

9
OVEREATERS ANONYMOUS

While I thought about my diet, I uncovered a lot of strong feelings that lay behind my overeating. Usually I could just tranquilize myself with food, but now I was the guinea pig for my own diet, so I had to deal with what was making me want to eat. I now knew that cutting calories wasn't the answer, personal awareness was. Two experiences convinced me to go to Overeaters Anonymous for Americans in Paris.

The first was with Joe in Harry's Bar. The maitre d' told us we'd have to wait an hour for a table, so we sat at the long bar. We drank Harry's special—freshly squeezed tomatoes and celery juice over ice. I ate a bowl of potato chips, then another and another. By the time I finished there wasn't a chip on the bar. The maitre d' told us we'd have to wait another fifteen minutes. I didn't care just as long as I could have more potato chips. I was asking the bartender for more when Lauren Hutton, looking breathtaking, walked in and told me, "Renée, don't eat potato chips. They're pure lard. Eat anything, but never that. *Never.*" Then she walked over to her friends who were waiting at a nearby table.

"What's the matter?" Joe asked when he saw my forlorn face.

"She told me I could *never* have potato chips," I said as though my best friend had just died. "I can live without alcohol, but I don't think I can make it through life without potato chips."

The other experience was at a buffet dinner party given by Joan Collins and her boyfriend Peter. Joe was still on the set and planned to join me at the party later, so I came early.

Sitting in the living room waiting for Joan and Peter to get dressed, I started nibbling on the tiny meatballs in the chafing dish on the dining room table. When Joan and Peter finally greeted me they screamed out to each other, "Where are the meatballs?"

"I'm sorry," I said. "I didn't realize it, but I must have eaten all of them."

"You ate meatballs for thirty people?" Joan asked incredulously.

"Really?" I said. "That's hard to believe."

I was so embarrassed the next day I went to my first OA meeting. You wouldn't think there were so many fat people in Paris, but when you consider the diet, you know why.

French Diet

Breakfast: Croissant
Pipérade (omelet with ham)
French coffee with sugar
Lunch: Vichyssoise (cream-of-potato soup)
French bread
Scallops in pastry
Brie cheese and fruit
Dinner: Onion soup with Camembert cheese
Chicken cordon bleu
Napoléon
French coffee with sugar

Of course, I never dreamed I was a compulsive overeater because I never got *that* fat. When I gained weight it was only 20 to 50 pounds, not like real overeaters. I thought it was just a "problem," not a disorder.

After going to Overeaters Anonymous, I realized I was a compulsive eater. I knew, because I ate when I felt bad. But then I would feel worse about what I had eaten. I ate when my cat was missing; I also ate when my cat was found. I never felt that I had enough. I had a strange attachment to food—even if it was old or not very good. I would enter a room, and if I knew there was cake there, I went crazy just knowing it. I would say to myself, "You can just have a taste." But I couldn't just taste. My "tastes" soon added up to four large pieces of cake.

Some people can eat a slice of apple pie or even two and then they forget about it. If I have one piece, I want the whole apple pie, then a blueberry and then a cherry pie. The craving has begun and there's no end—the obsession never ends. Overeating itself isn't a disease, but obsessive-compulsive eating is. You'll be happy to know it isn't contagious!

I knew I had to make a commitment to recovery and sanity, because what's more frightening about eating out of control is knowing that the *food* is in control. Foods jumped into my basket on their own in the supermarket. They must have, because I had amnesia attacks about how they got into my grocery bag.

At Overeaters Anonymous in Paris I didn't always understand the English because of their French accents, but the pain of not being able to stop eating was universal. Then I went to an OA meeting in Venice, when the cast went on location there a week later. The Italians seemed powerless over their disease too.

Italian Diet

Breakfast: Italian pastry
Espresso with sugar
Lunch: Antipasto (salami, anchovies, etc.)
Cannelloni
Italian bread

	Zuppa inglese (sponge cake, with ricotta and strawberries)
	Espresso with sugar
Dinner:	Veal Parmesan
	Spaghetti with clam sauce
	Ricotta cheesecake
	Espresso with sugar

All the years of dieting had screwed up my metabolism so that if I ate only three bowls of steam I still wouldn't lose. I was in such a state of denial about my compulsive eating that my fat resisted me and wouldn't come off. I had to discover a way to live that meant three meals a day and *life in between*. As soon as I got back home I asked my fat movie star friend to come with me to an Overeaters Anonymous meeting at Beverly Hills High School. She'd lost 15 pounds on my diet and had 85 more to go. But she didn't want to come along with me because she still insisted she wasn't a compulsive eater.

"What makes you think *I* am?" she said stuffing popcorn in her mouth.

"Stop eating that."

"It's a fruit."

"Popcorn is not a fruit," I said. "Particularly when it's buttered and salted. Look, the first step is to just admit you have an eating disorder. It's not your fault. Being obese is a disease."

"I don't consider myself obese."

"Well, what's your definition?"

"My definition of obese is anyone who weighs 20 pounds more than me. How do you know I'm even overweight?"

"Because whenever we go for a ride in your Rolls, I know why you don't fasten your seat belt—you can't. That tells me you're overweight. Come with me to Overeaters Anonymous. I want you to see that your fatness is not unique. There's a lot of us hiding out in Beverly Hills."

"Look, I don't want to go there, because God comes to

those people in stereo and he doesn't even broadcast FM to me."

"You don't have to use the G word at all at OA. Just pray to the part of you that's not Swiss cheese."

"I want to go to Switzerland and take the sleep cure. I'll wake up in two months and be thin," said my fat friend.

"You'd have to go for nine months. You're going to sleep away nine months of your life? Just grab onto my hand and say 'There's never been enough food for us, Renée. This time you and I are going to *make* our food *enough*.'" My fat friend just looked at me as though she were in a trance.

"What are you thinking about?" I asked.

"I'm thinking about your bagel. Are you going to leave half of it?"

"Come to the meeting. At least you won't eat for those two hours."

"Okay," she said. "Just let me turn off the potato that's in the oven."

Suddenly I understood why her house was always heated to 450°F. She always had a potato baking in the oven.

On the way to the high school, she insisted on stopping at a 7-Eleven for a double-chocolate milkshake. She needed to hold onto it for security. I was afraid she'd change her mind if I said anything about it, so I bit my tongue and said nothing. The other people at OA looked at her as though she were insane. Eating a milkshake at Overeaters Anonymous is like bringing booze to an Alcoholics Anonymous meeting. To top it all, my friend wore dark glasses because she was afraid of being recognized. So were one-third of the other people at the meeting. Being an ex-boozer or even a drug addict may be glamorous to some people, but being an ex-compulsive overeater is just "yucky."

We sat in a circle and everyone introduced themselves, "first names only." It was funny because we all pretended we didn't know each other. One star thanked her husband for giving up a football game to support her by coming that day. She was in a panic—she was nominated for an Academy

Award and couldn't get into her gown. She had gone from fear of failure to fear of success, from being an anorexic to sucking the juices from food and then spitting the rest out because her appetite had grown with her career. There was a well-known star director who had a bypass operation on his stomach. He lost over 200 pounds. Then they took out the bag inside him and he gained it all back.

I couldn't believe that a certain friend of mine was there. He had written a best-selling diet book, but he was so unnerved by his new success that he began to binge. He was terrified he would gain the weight back while he was on tour publicizing his book. He was first addicted to pizza and pepperoni and then he turned to cocaine to lose his appetite. He knew I cared about him, so after the meeting he asked me what to do with his obsession. I said, "Write another book on tour, about how you're distracting yourself from cocaine and pizza."

I thought how brave they all were to come out of the closet with their eating disorders. But then I came to understand that if the public should find out about them, so what? Their lives were in danger. Eating habits will only change when nothing else is as important as the commitment to giving up binges.

One woman who looked great turned out to be an old-timer. I asked what she did for a living, and she told me she was "in maintenance."

"What's that?"

"I'm maintaining my figure, my kids, my husband and my life because it's all good and I want to keep it that way."

My fat friend fell asleep at the meeting as soon as she finished her milkshake. I knew it was not from boredom—it was from fear. She knew the jig was up. She'd have to go cold turkey with her sugar binges.

There was another meeting starting in half an hour at Malibu. It was for "100 pounders"—people who had to lose 100 pounds, or who had already lost them and were trying to keep them off. I had heard it was a very inspiring meeting, and I told my fat friend this session would keep her awake. What surprised me the most about this OA group was that everyone looked normal. There were only three or four people over 100 pounds overweight. The rest looked like they needed to lose only 15 to 20 pounds.

I introduced myself and my friend (first names only), and they suggested she have a cup of coffee to stay awake. One woman got up and wrote on the blackboard "Fat Sucks," and the meeting began. Another beautiful woman told about when she weighed 100 pounds more and was sitting in a dentist's chair having root-canal work. The drill hit a nerve, and she was in so much agony she excused herself for a minute and ran out of the office to McDonald's for a double cheeseburger and french fries. That's how she knew she was a compulsive overeater—her instant comfort for pain was food. "Now," she said, "nothing tastes as good as abstinence feels."

The same woman said that when she was a child and she ate too much, she threw up, and her parents made her eat her own regurgitation to stop the habit. Her story was so sad that my fat friend and I cried practically the whole meeting. Then I stood up and said, "I'm Renée. I'm pretty sure I'm a compulsive overeater. I never wanted to admit it. I hoped it would go away. Drugs and alcohol you can hide; overeating can't be hidden. It just sits there. I tried counting calories but I would consume my calorie limit by 10:00 A.M. I realize that I've allowed demons to be in charge of my eating habits, and I'm here to slay dragons. You people have tremendous humility. It's a spiritual experience to be with you. I only have 60 pounds to lose, but I'd like to have a food sponsor who's lost 100 pounds to help me with the experiments I'm doing with my diet."

As soon as I sat down, a handsome young man tapped me on the shoulder.

"Renée, I would be happy to talk to you about what you should eat every day. I'm Jim, by the way."

I recognized him as a television star.

"Uh, hi, Jim. I thought a sponsor needed to be someone who was the same sex as me."

"That's only a suggestion," he said. "It really isn't necessary unless you think you'll have sexual fantasies when you abstain—you might feel less frightened if you share with someone of the same sex."

"I won't mind sharing with you even if I start fantasizing about sex with the Seven Dwarfs," I said. "What do you mean by abstaining, though?"

"You abstain from eating anything but three meals a day. They can be as big as you like, but you must commit to them in advance with me—you call them in every day. If you're about to binge between meals, you call."

"That's a lot of calls. Aren't you busy?"

"I'm a compulsive overeater, alcoholic and drug addict. When I came into the program, I weighed 272. I went from leading man to character actor. Now I'm back to romantic juvenile. If I help you, I help myself. Talking to you is talking to myself."

"It's wonderful to have support like this," I said.

"Here's my number. Call me anytime."

My fat friend said, "I got a seventy-five-year-old lady to sponsor me. I'm so jealous of who you got. I'm going right home to fantasize about having him on rye bread with mustard and sauerkraut."

"He is cute, isn't he?"

That night I called Jim.

"Have you taken inventory of your character defects?" he asked. "It's important to identify all the things that make you eat."

"I'll call you back."

It was very interesting to see how many defects I came up with.

I was *greedy*, wanting more than I needed, such as when I ate something in the refrigerator only because I didn't want anyone else to eat it. I *envied* the bulimics because their eating problem was so much worse than mine and they were forced to deal with it sooner. I was *slothful* because anytime during the day when I was uncomfortable I went to sleep to get away from the stress. I had too much *pride* to admit I was a compulsive overeater—I pretended I had a "weight problem." I was *jealous* of how much easier it was for other women to have their figures and their careers. I was *gluttonous,* because now I had become what Joan Crawford had suspected I was—a garbage eater, eating off other people's plates when I wasn't even hungry and then never "remembering" what I had eaten.

Then Joe and I were invited by Anna Strasberg to bring *It Had To Be You* to the Marilyn Monroe Theater at the Lee Strasberg Creative Center. It seemed like such a wonderful end to the cycle that began when I was a young actress in Lee's class with Marilyn. I had such good feelings about the production that it didn't bother me at all that although Burt Reynolds loved our screenplay, his studio had a new president who turned it down. Since it hadn't been written under his auspices, a rejection was par for the course. During that time, at Jim's suggestion, I began to swim an hour a day three times a week and do aerobic circuit training with an exercise trainer three times a week.

I have always been allergic to physical exercise because it's hard, and if you do it right, it hurts. However, when I saw the difference it made in my body, it was mind-boggling. Exercising shook up my unconscious mind so much that I felt new levels of awareness. I was exhausted and dripping wet after the workout. I didn't dare binge because I had worked so hard and I knew what the food would cost me in workout sweat. My appetite shrank a lot. I became more aware of what the real size of my stomach was and how little food it actually needed. I also gave up diet sodas at Morgan Fairchild's suggestion. At a cocktail party I saw her drinking from a champagne glass.

"What are you drinking?" I asked.
"White tea. I drink it all day."
"Where do you get white tea?"

"From the tap. You boil it. You pour it over ice and you have white tea."

"Water? You drink water all day?"

"It's good for the skin and the figure and it costs nothing. I don't like mineral water. The minerals hold onto the fat," she said.

Jim had me call in my food and commit my meal plan to him every day. One day Joe and I went to the Golden Globe Awards dinner because Joe was nominated for best supporting actor for *My Favorite Year*. They were serving a seven-course meal, but I had already eaten my daily food allotment before I left the house so I wouldn't be tempted.

Everyone was drinking champagne with fresh peach juice at the cocktail hour. I noticed Linda Evans had a cube of brown sugar floating in her glass. I ran to the phone to call Jim.

"My feelings of envy are overwhelming."

"Look how far you've come on your diet, Renée. Think of all the good things that have happened to you."

I went back to the cocktail party and ordered Évian water and lime. I saw Charlene Tilton wolfing down caviar on crackers with eggs and sour cream. I ran to the phone.

"I can't stand it, Jim. I'm feeling sorry for myself. Charlene Tilton is a size two and she's sucking up caviar like a vacuum cleaner."

"I'm so proud that you called. You're really getting in touch with your Higher Power. That's how I know you're going to make it on the program."

"How? I don't follow."

"For all the people that you're going to help by committing yourself to your diet and altering it until it works. You're learning to love something more than yourself."

I was excited by what he was saying. I put myself in my Higher Power's hands and went to find Joe sitting at our table. One of Hollywood's biggest superstars sat next to me. Everyone else at the table ate lamb in a pastry shell. She ordered broiled fish. I sat there with a forced smile on my lips, drinking water. Once more, I got up from the table to call Jim for courage.

"Jim, my knuckles are white from biting on them. Can't I just have a piece of fish like the woman sitting next to me is having? I'm not ready to be totally spiritual yet."

"There is no way to get ready to be spiritual. You become spiritual by becoming spiritual. Close your eyes. Ask your Higher Power for help, breathe in and out deeper and deeper, and your appetite will fade."

Back at the table I closed my eyes and breathed deeply in and out. When I opened my eyes, the woman next to me whispered, "Isn't Overeaters Anonymous wonderful? I used to go for my bulimia."

On the way home, Joe asked, "Who did you have to call in the middle of dinner?"

"My sponsor, Jim, from Overeaters."

"Oh, yeah?" Joe said. "You know how I love food. I don't like you sharing that with another man. It's too personal."

I loved it that he was jealous.

10
THE OTHER WOMAN

Then something happened for the first time in the twenty years that Joe and I had been together. Our relationship was threatened.

I always trusted Joe because I had no reason not to. His love had been tested a hundred times over, inadvertently, and each time he came through with flying colors. I have always called him my "boyfriend," and I introduced him to people that way too. It's the highest honor I can pay him, because having a boyfriend means everything to me. I never had a real one until I met him, and I had longed for one since I was eleven. Even when I hated him, or worse, when I was so angry with him that I was indifferent or turned off to him, I knew it would pass because deep down he'd always be my permanent boyfriend.

I'm telling you all this so you'll understand the secure state of mind I was in when I met the Other Woman. It all started innocently enough. Joe and I were in rehearsal for *It Had To Be You* in Hollywood. Joe was to start shooting a film in Los Angeles after we opened. He'd be in the movie during the day and our play at night. I was busy going to Overeaters Anonymous during my lunch hour and before the play, with Jim. I was starting to be a recovering foodaholic, and I began making notes of things to discuss with Jim—insights about my weight problem, such as:

1. I didn't know the difference between cure of my fatness and control of my fatness. I might never cure my need to be fat but I could still control it.
2. Fasting or feasting were always easy for me, but I scoffed at control because I thought it was "nothing."
3. When I ate fast I was trying to fill up my feeling of deprivation, which was a bottomless well. (Actually, it was my deprivation and my mother's, so I was eating for two.)
4. I wanted a magical cure to lose weight and keep it off. I didn't want to have to do it myself.
5. My huge appetite wasn't really for food, but for acknowledgment.
6. Getting up in the middle of the night to weigh myself was not constructive, it was compulsive.
7. I don't have to be thin *before* I abstain.
8. The way for me to get thin is to eat three meals a day, twenty minutes each, and have as much as I want of my allotted foods. Then I get up from the table and eat nothing in between.
9. I don't have to be sane to believe in a Higher Power.
10. You can't remove your hunger on your own terms by making it disappear. You have to work with the hunger you've been given by the Life Force, and learn to harness it.
11. I don't know the difference between bingeing and normal eating because I was always on a binge.
12. I judge whether I'm having a good time at a party by what I eat, and at a restaurant by how large the portions are.

I was preoccupied with these thoughts, so I didn't notice Joe's reaction to the Other Woman. We met her at a party given by the producer for all the people connected with the movie. The Other Woman was a beautiful international film star with a perfect, voluptuous body.

"I heard about you. You don't cheat on your wife," she said to Joe sneeringly, in her French accent. She said it as though it were an insult. Joe laughed as if it were a joke.

"That's me," he answered nervously.
"Can I ask you a personal question?" I asked.
"Who are you?"
"I'm his wife. What do you eat? I'd be very interested in trying out your diet because you look so terrific."
"Julio says my looks come from swimming two hours twice a week. Yves says my looks come from aerobics two hours twice a week. But Charles says my looks come from my daily ice cream."
"Julio?" I asked.
"Julio Iglesias."
"Yves?"
"Yves Montand."
"Charles?"
"Charles Aznavour." She was dating some international hot stuff.
"Ice cream?"
"I diet on ice cream."
"How can that be?"
"I get to have what's forbidden every day by giving myself a tease of ice cream."
"A teaspoon?"
"No, a tease is much more. It's half a cup."

The Other Woman's Diet

½ cup of French ice cream six times a day.
(180 calories × 6 = 1080 calories per day)

"I lose 8 pounds a week this way," she said. "If you want to lose more, eat American ice cream. One half cup is only 145 calories per day. But the French is more nutritious because it has egg yolk in it."

Can you imagine, she lost weight on ice cream? I was so envious of her diet that I didn't notice how much Joe was taken with her being taken with him.

One night a few weeks later the phone rang and I picked it up.

"Halloo, is *he* there?" she asked in her French accent.

"He *who?*" I pretended I didn't know what she was talking about.

"He, *Joe*," she said sneeringly.

"I don't know," I said sneeringly back to her. "I'll ask him. Joe, are you here?" I handed him the phone.

I didn't like her treating me as though I wasn't there.

"Hello," he said. Then as he heard her voice, I saw him blush. "Uh-huh. Uh-huh. Uh-huh. Sure. I'll be right over."

"I have to go, Renée. She's frightened to death of the love scenes in the movie and she wants to rehearse at her house without the pressure of a shooting schedule and the whole crew standing around watching her in the nude."

"In the nude?" I said, my voice going up three octaves. "You're going to rehearse with her in the nude? What does that have to do with acting?"

"Look," he said, trying to make a joke, "your problem has always been inhibitions. You don't have any. She does. She needs to go through the feelings of acting with no clothes on."

"We don't know what my inhibitions are. I walk around the house naked in front of you because you love me. I don't think I could or would do it on the screen, because I don't think it's necessary. If I were ever asked, I'd say it's too personal. I can share all of myself but that. Let her use a naked double in the love scene if she's so inhibited she has to practice."

"You're scaring me. I don't know what to make of this. Could you come along to her house and watch us rehearse?" he asked.

"I'd rather not. It puts me in the role of being your mother. You go alone. I'll trust you. Just think of me when you're kissing her and kiss her like this," I said, kissing him passionately, but with my mouth closed and my eyes open. I could tell Joe was starting to panic.

"Please come. I'm starting to feel inhibited myself, and

maybe you can give me some acting tips to loosen me up." He knew that would appeal to me. I've always been interested in character *behavior* in acting scenes, so I went. I was also jealous, not because she was breathtakingly beautiful, but because, with all her inhibition baloney, I knew she was hot for Joe. Hot, beautiful and amoral is a tough combination to beat.

We went over to her house high on a hill in Bel Air. She was surprised to see me but she pretended the whole session was only about her acting, even though she greeted us in a black sheer robe with ruffled nightgown underneath.

They started to go through their lines. She was searching for her "motivation." They started kissing. I noticed that his lips were closed tight and that her arms had no fat on them at all like mine did. I wanted to ask what exercise she did for that. I also wanted to ask why she needed this rehearsal to find the "free spirit" that was her character, when she was so "wildly free" herself. I wished she could give me lessons in how to be the way she was—so sensual, so sexual, so confidently entitled to seduce whomever she wanted.

"Here I am," she said, speaking her line from the script. Then she stood up and dropped her nightgown. I gasped. Joe stared in disbelief. That was the body I had always wanted. It was so perfect. Her bosom. Her hips. Her thighs. I wondered if she'd had plastic surgery. I wanted to believe that it had all been sanded down, built up and possibly moved. I decided it was inappropriate to ask her then and there. As impulsively as she had pulled off her gown, she put it back up on her shoulders.

"No, I can't take off my clothes," she said, now out of character, to Joe. "It brings up my childhood. My brothers always made fun of my large bosom, so I can't be naked in this scene."

"Then don't be," I volunteered.

"Joe, I can't perform in front of your wife. She makes me nervous." She punctuated her words with a pout.

"I'm not watching you as his wife. I'm watching you as an artist."

"Unless you leave, I won't be able to play my part in this movie," she paused. "I said unless you leave—"

"I heard you," I said. "May I ask you a personal question? What exercise do you use to firm up your arms?"

"How dare you! How dare you!" I think that was the translation of what she said to me in French. Anyway, I left. A few minutes later Joe followed me out to the street.

"How am I going to get through this picture with her?" he asked on the ride home. "She's so oversensitive."

"Look Joe, you're going to be wonderful in this movie no matter what, and I think I just figured out the secret to weight loss. My idea for a great new diet is based on her ice cream tease," I said excitedly.

Then I began to formulate the diet based on the principle that if I was already bingeing in a controlled way, my forbidden foods didn't have to be forbidden any longer. I would give myself all the things I loved during the space of a week and then I would have no reason to go off my diet.

Jim said, "Don't do it. You're playing with fire. Anyway, not if you want me to be your sponsor."

"Jim, it's my food. And my body, remember that."

"Our body, Renée. We both have the same problem. I'm only sharing what's worked for me."

"Jim, I need more freedom to experiment. I want to try more fruits. I want to see if I can have pasta three times a day. And if I'll gain on veal. But most of all, I must know if I can eat ice cream one day a week and still lose," I said.

"I can't be a party to anything but the moderate OA eating plan. Call me if you're willing to commit rigorously to one of the plans that OA recommends," Jim said.

I felt abandoned, but I had to find out about my own body for myself.

One day I ate only fruit all day—six different kinds and nothing else. I lost a pound.

The next day, I had pasta at all three meals. I lost a pound. (I made it with artichoke pasta since I'm allergic to wheat.)

For steak day, I had it three times. I lost a pound. (I used organic meat from the health food store.)

On my ice cream day, I ate it all day. I lost 1 pound. (I made it with fructose and fruit juice since I'm allergic to sugar.)

It became very clear to me what the natural principles of the Taylor-Made Diet should be. I discovered that if I ate one course of a seven-course meal each day of the week for three weeks I could lose 15 to 21 pounds, depending on how much weight had to be lost and how salt free I was willing to stay. After the third week I could begin week one again. The best thing about this plan was that it allowed me to eat all my favorite foods.

Here is the schedule that I worked out:

Week One

Tuesday:	Fruit
Wednesday:	Grain
Thursday:	Salad
Friday:	Fowl
Saturday:	Vegetables
Sunday:	Eggs, fish, meat
Monday:	Dessert

Week Two

Tuesday:	Eggs and Meat
Wednesday:	Salad
Thursday:	Fish
Friday:	Fruit
Saturday:	Grain
Sunday:	Vegetables
Monday:	Dessert

Week Three

Tuesday: Meat
Wednesday: Salad
Thursday: Chicken or eggs, and fish
Friday: Fruit
Saturday: Grain
Sunday: Vegetables
Monday: Dessert

Best of all, I lost weight! I started to look different and people noticed. Joe and I opened *It Had to Be You* to rave reviews in Los Angeles. We had two opening-night parties because so many friends and celebrities wanted to see the play. I felt it was a real triumph for me, and it made up for everything. The Other Woman came to both parties and followed Joe around like a puppy dog. She seemed to be high on something, blabbing away about how fame and money meant nothing to her in her $6,000 Giorgio gown and her $2,500 Judith Leber rhinestone bag shaped like Buddha. (Buddha must have been rolling over in his grave.)

"All I want is the love of a good man," she said.

"Ha, ha, ha. That's right," I wanted to say, because the "good man" was Joe.

I think Joe was very aroused by her pursuit of him but he wouldn't admit it. Then her ex-husband and her child showed up at our second party. She had left them to live with a superstar who had abused her and eventually thrown her out. It seemed the ex-husband and the child "inhibited" her too. She was certainly the most seductive victim I had ever met.

At the party, holding the child in his arms, her ex-husband slapped her, and she began to sob hysterically in French. She ruined my second opening-night party—after this scene the guests all left early. She was sobbing all over the dessert tray, but that didn't kill her taste buds. I counted the desserts she ate. Six. The chocolate mousse, the chocolate cheesecake, two chocolate brownies, a chocolate after-dinner mint and a chocolate-covered petit four.

"What happened to your ice cream diet?" I asked.

"I'm on my chocolate cake week now," she said, wiping the tears from her cheeks.

Noticing my envious look, she said, "Are you happy with the way you look? As a friend I tell you, you should lose about 60 pounds."

"Are you happy with the way you look? As your friend I'm telling you, you could *use* the 60," I said, feeling hurt. I was lying. The Duchess of Windsor said, "You can never be too rich or too thin," but the Other Woman *was* too thin. Unfortunately, on her it looked sexy.

Chocolate cake *week!* I never heard of such a thing. I noticed how round and firm her ass was in her red satin slip gown.

The next day I tried cake all day. I gained back half a pound. She must be up all night exercising or screwing—how else could she lose with her eating patterns? I called my exercise trainer and asked him if he would work with me *every day*. I wanted to firm my arms and my behind like hers.

I was going to Overeaters Anonymous every day now while Joe filmed the movie. I heard real horror stories at OA. One woman ate wood, sponges, everything but nails. She even tried to eat the phone and the keys on the piano. She was afraid her mother would make her eat these things if she didn't eat her vegetables, so she ate them first. She literally ate her family out of house and home! I considered myself lucky to just be a compulsive overeater.

Then I ran into Jim. He looked like he had just gained 50 pounds.

"What happened?" I asked.

"I've been on a sugar binge since you got rid of me as your sponsor. I really shouldn't be at this meeting. I had two Fudgsicles before I came tonight. I was very attached to you, and you let me down just like my mother did. I was her favorite and one day she dumped me at the orphanage."

"I'm so sorry. I had no idea. At least you have your work."

"I've been canned because of my weight."

That's when I got the idea to fix him up with my fat friend, who was beginning to lose weight.

"She's been abstinent on my diet for three months and she's very rigid about it. Why don't you let her sponsor you?" I said.

I was happy I'd made a match. Eventually he moved in with her and they were the first couple to be on the cover of *213*, the Beverly Hills magazine, where the *woman* was twenty-five years older than the man.

Then about two weeks into the shooting of his movie Joe came to me in a lot of pain.

"She's in love with me, Renée. What am I going to do?"

"What is she eating?"

"Who cares? That's beside the point."

"It's exactly the point to me," I said. "I know her eating habits when she's on the make and when she's on the town. Now I want to know what she eats when she's in love."

Whatever she was eating, it agreed with her. She never looked better than she did sitting at my kitchen table the next morning popping pills in her mouth.

"What's that?" I asked.

"Saccharin. Whenever I crave something sweet, I chew saccharin. It has such an unpleasant aftertaste I lose my cravings."

"Really." I wondered if that was true or if she was chewing speed.

"Would you like to hear a joke that's going around Hollywood? How does a wife get revenge when her husband cheats? She gets fatter and fatter. And what does a wife do when she's about to leave her husband? She gets thinner and thinner."

"That is funny. I may be getting thinner but I have no intention of leaving Joe, not while we make love three times a week. Sometimes on the kitchen table, the pool table, the marble cocktail table. Tables turn me on," I added, trying to make her jealous.

"You're toning up your arms, I see." She pretended not to hear what I said. "You know, I worry about Joe—he needs to build up his breastplate. And you should do my exercise for your chin—pull it tightly backward. It's a face lift without surgery. I've been doing it for ten years, so I have no double chin."

"It's sweet of you to worry about Joe's breastplate. How old are you?"

"Thirty-five."

She looked younger. (I've heard that really disturbed people like schizophrenics don't age.)

"But please don't tell Joe."

"Why not?"

"He needs a younger woman," she answered.

"You mean younger than *you?* He would never need a woman younger than me. There is no one younger. I feel younger than when I was thirteen. I started out feeling old because I was pressured to achieve, and as I suffered, I got younger."

"I mean younger than *you*, not me," she said.

Joe was shooting a scene without her that day, and she had dropped by to give me this good news.

"Could I ask you a personal question?"

"Of course," she said.

"I asked Joe, but he said he didn't care. What are you eating this week?"

"You are stupid. So stupid. I am telling you Joe needs a younger woman than you and you ask me what I eat," she said, getting into a self-righteous snit as only the French can.

"You are so wrong. Joe always promised me if he ever fell in love with someone else she wouldn't be younger. It would be someone older who's a much *deeper* person than me. Someone like Mother Teresa."

"Joe loves me, you fool," she said.

"You're mistaken."

"He held me in his arms and told me. Ask. Ask him."

"I will if you tell me what you've been eating this week." I agreed because I wasn't sure how else to handle the situation.

"Veggies," she sneered. "This week my body craves veggies. Monday: escarole. Tuesday: brussels sprouts. Wednesday: celery root. Thursday: broccoli. Friday: pumpkin squash. Saturday: Chinese cabbage. Sunday: eggplant. I eat as much as I want every day, and if I want to indulge myself, I chew saccharin. Now, will you ask him?" she screamed.

"After I try the veggies," I screamed back, stalling for time.

"You're obsessed with your diet. That's how you drove him into my arms." She grabbed her purple running jacket triumphantly and stormed out.

I suddenly realized how color coordinated she was—pink sneakers, gray leg warmers, mauve tights, eggplant leotards and deep-purple satin jacket. From my window I watched her climb into her black Mercedes convertible with violet upholstery. It was more than I could bear. She was right. I had become obsessed with my diet. It gave spiritual meaning to my existence.

It was becoming a metaphor for life. My total focus was on recreating myself 2 pounds underweight. Joan of Arc never paid attention to the pettiness of her army—she kept her eye on the Battle of Orléans. And I wasn't going to pay attention to Joe and the Other Woman or the ups and downs of my Hollywood career anymore. My eye was on the Battle of Losing 60 Pounds by tonight, one day at a time. Thinking that way, victory was in sight! I would lose weight and keep it off. My triumph would be Mind over my Matter.

I ate vegetables that day. One at each meal. I wrote in my food diary: string beans for breakfast, spinach for lunch, Chinese cabbage for dinner. That night when Joe came home I asked him casually, "Did you tell her you were in love with her?"

"I did."

"Then it's over between us. My blood has run cold. It doesn't mean I don't love you. I just feel betrayed. It's nothing personal. I would feel this way toward any man who loved *her*."

"Wait a minute. I didn't mean romantic love. I meant love like compassion."

"Look, tell me the truth. If you do love her sexually, it's okay. Have her and I'll get someone else for our play. It's no big deal. I have Gabriel. I have my diet. I'll be okay, but you can't be my boyfriend anymore."

"I swear this is what happened. She came to work with black and blue marks on her arms and thighs and said her ex-husband roughed her up when he caught her with Mick Jagger at the Beverly Wilshire Hotel. I felt sorry for her."

"But you hate Mick Jagger. How could you feel sorry for her?"

"She threw herself at him because she was trying to forget about me. She feels close to me, and I haven't shared anything with her. Don't you feel compassion for her? She's sitting outside in her car. I told her it was okay to come over to talk it all out. She's upset."

"She's upset? Oh, then bring her in by all means."

Joe waved to her, and in she came in a tight red leather pants suit with matching cowboy fringe and boots. She knew what to wear for every occasion. Suddenly I hated the navy blue Jane Fonda workout clothes that I had on.

"Thank you for inviting me in. I'm going to have my fa[ce] peeled tomorrow, and my doctor says I must be calm bef[ore] my surgery," she said.

"Why are you peeling your face?"

"It takes off the wrinkles."

"Where are the wrinkles?"

"There's one here," she pointed under her right eye, one over here," pointing under her left eye.

"Oh, yeah," I said. "But they give you character[. Don't] you want to have character?"

"What I want is to look perfect."

"You do already," Joe said, trying to be nice.

"What's so good about perfection? Day in and d[ay out,] boring anyway," I said.

"He wants me, and I deserve a good man for a change. We're going away to screw our heads off right after my peeling," she said.

"What makes you say that?" Joe asked.

"I know you want me and you want to screw me, don't you? Tell her," she demanded.

She said "screw" like it was a great food she was starved for.

"Okay, Joe, let's hear," I said.

"I want to screw her."

"Oh, my God. You were going to be a priest when you were young. I married you because I thought you'd always be faithful."

"I will be. I'm just telling you that I want to."

"Who cares? I want to screw a lot of people. I don't go around telling them, nor do I tell you. You're fixating on this woman and it's annoying, particularly since she's an international movie star. If you had picked Doris Schwartz, a regular person like me, it would have been fairer. Making the fantasy real is unfair, Joe. I'm only an average crazy person trying to have a life. I'm trying to invent a new diet to control my binges so I can control my weight. Give up your preoccupation with her. It's causing you anxiety. It's causing me anx- Tell yourself she's gorgeous, she's hot, she's amoral. So

me. Help me," he answered.

is not a preoccupation." She sneered at me as popping open the top snap on her skin-tight boy jacket as she clenched her teeth. "It's only if it's not consummated. I *want* to consum-

ght she was disgusting, I envied her what she was doing, not that I would to know I was capable of it. I'd never ever make this diet book into a ven get to do my part if they make I was "miscast" again.

"Listen, bitch. You've shared a lot of secrets about nutrition and I thank you, but you come on to Joe one more time and you won't have to have your skin peeled because I'll peel it for you."

"You're nothing. He wants me and I'm going to have him now," she snarled.

"Okay, girlie," I said, pulling her by her cheeks and dragging her across the floor. It was hard work, because even though she was underweight and thinner than me, she was *muscular* and it felt like I was dragging a boulder through the house.

"I'm sorry," Joe said after she left. "I didn't know what was happening. How can you ever forgive me?"

I thought for a long time.

"I don't know. But first, you're going to have to exorcise her from your fantasy and fall madly and hotly in love with me."

I'd heard that after twenty years together, couples often have real problems with their relationships. The reason is that in the process of loving each other we play so many roles—lover, wife, sister, friend, mother, father, child. You can be sister to his father, or father to his sister and so on, in dozens of combinations. Then after twenty years you run out of things to "be" to each other.

Our twentieth anniversary was approaching, and I decided that the way for our relationship to flower again was to begin all over and be reborn as lovers. Not long after the scene with the Other Woman, I called Joe on the phone. "You don't know me, but I saw you running on the beach at Santa Monica and I love your thighs. I've got to kiss them."

"Who is this?"

"Meet me tonight at eight at the Beverly Comstock Hotel. Room 305 and you'll find out."

"Renée, is that you?"

"Maybe yes, maybe no. Why? Did I get you hot?"

"Yes. I never got an obscene phone call before."

"So are you going to meet me at the hotel?"

At the Beverly Comstock Joe and I played a charade that we've repeated many times in hotel lobbies all over the world. He sits in a chair reading the paper. I pretend to be a hooker. I pick him up by saying, "Do you want to go upstairs and have some fun?"

"I can't. I'm married."

"I'm embroiled myself. You tell me about your bitch. I'll tell you about my bastard."

Then we go upstairs and I tell him about all my resentments toward him and vice versa. We don't get mad because we each try to have the same amount of empathy that a stranger would. We also get to have the fun of feeling as if we're starting an illicit love affair.

Once at the Plaza Hotel when we played the pickup game, a detective asked me to leave the premises. "We've had a lot of complaints about you."

"Officer, this is a game we're playing. This man is really my husband."

"Is that true?" the detective asked Joe.

"I never saw her before in my life."

The detective led me out of the lobby, but I enjoyed the whole thing. I felt that I had finally made the grade with my diet if I could be mistaken for a hooker.

Another game we played at the Beverly Hills Hotel was showing each other the kind of sex we were going to have with the next person we "picked up." It was very liberating to think of us as being involved in a totally sexual encounter.

personal. I would feel this way toward any man who loved *her*."

"Wait a minute. I didn't mean romantic love. I meant love like compassion."

"Look, tell me the truth. If you do love her sexually, it's okay. Have her and I'll get someone else for our play. It's no big deal. I have Gabriel. I have my diet. I'll be okay, but you can't be my boyfriend anymore."

"I swear this is what happened. She came to work with black and blue marks on her arms and thighs and said her ex-husband roughed her up when he caught her with Mick Jagger at the Beverly Wilshire Hotel. I felt sorry for her."

"But you hate Mick Jagger. How could you feel sorry for her?"

"She threw herself at him because she was trying to forget about me. She feels close to me, and I haven't shared anything with her. Don't you feel compassion for her? She's sitting outside in her car. I told her it was okay to come over to talk it all out. She's upset."

"She's upset? Oh, then bring her in by all means."

Joe waved to her, and in she came in a tight red leather pants suit with matching cowboy fringe and boots. She knew what to wear for every occasion. Suddenly I hated the navy blue Jane Fonda workout clothes that I had on.

"Thank you for inviting me in. I'm going to have my face peeled tomorrow, and my doctor says I must be calm before my surgery," she said.

"Why are you peeling your face?"

"It takes off the wrinkles."

"Where are the wrinkles?"

"There's one here," she pointed under her right eye. "And one over here," pointing under her left eye.

"Oh, yeah," I said. "But they give you character. Don't you want to have character?"

"What I want is to look perfect."

"You do already," Joe said, trying to be nice.

"What's so good about perfection? Day in and day out, it's boring anyway," I said.

"He wants me, and I deserve a good man for a change. We're going away to screw our heads off right after my peeling," she said.

"What makes you say that?" Joe asked.

"I know you want me and you want to screw me, don't you? Tell her," she demanded.

She said "screw" like it was a great food she was starved for.

"Okay, Joe, let's hear," I said.

"I want to screw her."

"Oh, my God. You were going to be a priest when you were young. I married you because I thought you'd always be faithful."

"I will be. I'm just telling you that I want to."

"Who cares? I want to screw a lot of people. I don't go around telling them, nor do I tell you. You're fixating on this woman and it's annoying, particularly since she's an international movie star. If you had picked Doris Schwartz, a regular person like me, it would have been fairer. Making the fantasy real is unfair, Joe. I'm only an average crazy person trying to have a life. I'm trying to invent a new diet to control my binges so I can control my weight. Give up your preoccupation with her. It's causing you anxiety. It's causing me anxiety. Tell yourself she's gorgeous, she's hot, she's amoral. So what!"

"Help me. Help me," he answered.

"Our love is not a preoccupation." She sneered at me as only she could, popping open the top snap on her skin-tight red leather cowboy jacket as she clenched her teeth. "It's only a preoccupation if it's not consummated. I *want* to consummate it. Now."

Even though I thought she was disgusting, I envied her nerve. I could never do what she was doing, not that I would want to, but I'd just like to know I was capable of it. I'd never get to do her part if they ever make this diet book into a movie. I'll probably never even get to do my part if they make this into a movie. They'll say I was "miscast" again.

"Listen, bitch. You've shared a lot of secrets about nutrition and I thank you, but you come on to Joe one more time and you won't have to have your skin peeled because I'll peel it for you."

"You're nothing. He wants me and I'm going to have him now," she snarled.

"Okay, girlie," I said, pulling her by her cheeks and dragging her across the floor. It was hard work, because even though she was underweight and thinner than me, she was *muscular* and it felt like I was dragging a boulder through the house.

"I'm sorry," Joe said after she left. "I didn't know what was happening. How can you ever forgive me?"

I thought for a long time.

"I don't know. But first, you're going to have to exorcise her from your fantasy and fall madly and hotly in love with me."

I'd heard that after twenty years together, couples often have real problems with their relationships. The reason is that in the process of loving each other we play so many roles—lover, wife, sister, friend, mother, father, child. You can be sister to his father, or father to his sister and so on, in dozens of combinations. Then after twenty years you run out of things to "be" to each other.

Our twentieth anniversary was approaching, and I decided that the way for our relationship to flower again was to begin all over and be reborn as lovers. Not long after the scene with the Other Woman, I called Joe on the phone. "You don't know me, but I saw you running on the beach at Santa Monica and I love your thighs. I've got to kiss them."

"Who is this?"

"Meet me tonight at eight at the Beverly Comstock Hotel. Room 305 and you'll find out."

"Renée, is that you?"

"Maybe yes, maybe no. Why? Did I get you hot?"

"Yes. I never got an obscene phone call before."

"So are you going to meet me at the hotel?"

At the Beverly Comstock Joe and I played a charade that we've repeated many times in hotel lobbies all over the world. He sits in a chair reading the paper. I pretend to be a hooker. I pick him up by saying, "Do you want to go upstairs and have some fun?"

"I can't. I'm married."

"I'm embroiled myself. You tell me about your bitch. I'll tell you about my bastard."

Then we go upstairs and I tell him about all my resentments toward him and vice versa. We don't get mad because we each try to have the same amount of empathy that a stranger would. We also get to have the fun of feeling as if we're starting an illicit love affair.

Once at the Plaza Hotel when we played the pickup game, a detective asked me to leave the premises. "We've had a lot of complaints about you."

"Officer, this is a game we're playing. This man is really my husband."

"Is that true?" the detective asked Joe.

"I never saw her before in my life."

The detective led me out of the lobby, but I enjoyed the whole thing. I felt that I had finally made the grade with my diet if I could be mistaken for a hooker.

Another game we played at the Beverly Hills Hotel was showing each other the kind of sex we were going to have with the next person we "picked up." It was very liberating to think of us as being involved in a totally sexual encounter.

11
LEAN AND SERENE AT LAST

Now my food week was all laid out. During our Los Angeles play run I made my goal. I lost 62 more pounds on the diet.

I had a strange reaction to losing all my excess weight plus 2 pounds to make me underweight. When I looked down at the scale and saw that it registered 112, I nonchalantly walked downstairs to the kitchen and had a cup of coffee. Then it hit me what a miracle this was. Could it really be true? This was the culmination of a whole lifetime of screwing around with food. It had led me to this year's program on the Taylor-Made Diet—*and it worked!*

I ran back up the stairs to the bathroom and weighed myself again. It was true—*112!* When it really hit me that I actually weighed *112*, diet doctors, nutritionists and the food itself no longer had any power over me. At *112 pounds* I took the power back. I'm now in control of my body and I'm keeping it that way. What I am now is what I will become. I am thin. I am going to be thin. I say this every morning when I wake up, at mealtimes and when I go to sleep. I've written it down and stuck it on my mirror, my refrigerator, my car dashboard and all over the house. I am thin and I am going to be thin.

I called my fat friend and told her to do it.

"But I haven't made my weight."

"Here's how to make your weight sooner. Change your

"That was Catherine Deneuve."

I was sure I would drop dead in the next few minutes, because all my dreams were coming true.

On my second wedding day I wore a floor-length white lace gown with iridescent sequins and a bridal veil, by Rina di Montella. Joe and the ushers were in black tie, and my bridesmaids wore black tulle gowns and floppy black hats with white roses pinned to them. I carried two dozen long-stemmed white roses tied with a satin bow. The tables were decorated with black cloths and black vases and white roses. It was the elegant wedding I wanted twenty years ago when we were first married, and I was so happy to have it now.

We were going to have the ceremony at our house, but when the invitation list reached 350, our producer friends, Fay and Aaron Schwab, offered their huge estate on Sunset Boulevard. We opened our home to all our friends and relatives who couldn't afford to stay at hotels. Every bed and couch in the house was taken, and I added four beds in the garage for my cousin Charlotte Lang's teenage boys. We put blankets over the windows in the living room because I didn't want my neighbors to see that we had turned the place into a boarding house.

Joe's relatives Carmel and Vinnie Altomare came from New Jersey to decorate the "hoopa" with white roses, and his Aunt Bea brought her own pan from Brooklyn to make the lasagna. His cousin Mary Jean Badalementi made three different kinds of pasta: tortellini, primavera and puttanesca. For my Jewish relatives, I ordered chopped liver molded into a heart and potato knishes shaped like roses from Canter's Restaurant. The wedding cake had a bride and groom standing under a huppah, all made of white chocolate. Kids from Gabriel's tap-dancing school, Pat Rico's, entertained at the wedding, and friends of Joe's from college and from his days playing the Catskills sang and did comedy.

My matron of honor was my fat movie star friend, who was no longer fat. She had lost 115 pounds on my diet. By then, she was engaged to Jim, who was back on his television series after the *Enquirer* told the whole shocking truth about his being fired because of the 50-pound Fudgsicle episode. And you'll never guess who was my maid of honor. I invited her only because I was in such a state of bliss from staying on my diet and being abstinent from binges for a year, that I was just inviting anyone I'd ever known. But to tell you the truth, I never dreamed she'd come.

"I just received your wedding invitation, and it sounds so wonderful. 'Renée and Joe Bologna invite you to share three of the four mutual passions that have held their marriage together: classic Italian cuisine, Jewish deli and laughter,'" she read off the invitation. "I would love to be in the bridal party," the Other Woman said on the phone.

"You would?" I was shocked. I wanted to ask, "What for?" but I thought it would be ungracious. Maybe she was sorry she came on to Joe, or maybe she missed me and wanted to tell me more about her diet. Maybe she had read in Jody Jacobs' society column that practically "everybody in Hollywood was talking about" our coming nuptials. So out of nervousness, or guilt that I didn't even want her there, like a jerk, I said, "You want to be my maid of honor?"

When she said, "It would mean everything to me," I thought I'd die, because now I was stuck with her.

I went to Overeaters Anonymous three times in one day to talk about it. Just like someone coming off drugs still suffers from drug behavior and someone who stops drinking is still considered a "dry drunk," I still considered myself to be a struggling abstinent overeater.

When I was a child, the movies were bigger and better than life. Now I had grown up to create my life to be bigger and better than a movie. I gave myself everything I had ever wanted: a perfect figure, a loving husband and child, and a fairy-tale wedding with all the stars in Hollywood who were my childhood idols in attendance.

Then I went and invited the Other Woman to be in my wedding party. I wasn't scared about being compared to her gorgeous looks. What scared me was the question of why, with my new full life, I had added the anxiety of including a sado-masochistic scene stealer in my wedding party.

Then I had an insight as to why I did it. I felt *sorry* for the Other Woman because I had taken Joe away from her, even though he was my husband. It reminded me of my childhood. My mother was so pretty. I suppose I repressed my desire to be prettier so I could take my father away from her one day. Even with this two-bit psychology lesson, I felt trapped about having her as maid of honor. I put off telling Joe until the last minute because I knew he'd be upset. Instead, he said, "I know why you did it. You look so much sexier than her now." Go figure. He was as hot for me as he had been for her.

I prayed that I wouldn't binge my brains out from stress on my wedding day. The fantastic dinner was all seven courses of my diet for the week, on seven small buffet tables. At least two dozen of my friends who attended were on my diet, and I made it easy for them to stay on it at the affair. There was fruit, salad, baked chicken, vegetables, three kinds of pasta, broiled fish and three kinds of fruit-juice cakes. For the people who weren't on any diet, I had cheese blintzes, salt bagels, chopped liver, salami, pastrami and hot dogs. I asked Jim to hang around the table and hand out Overeaters Anonymous brochures.

The night before, we had a wedding rehearsal with the eight bridesmaids and eight ushers. At the last minute the Other Woman canceled.

"Please forgive me. I can't come."

"To the wedding?" I said excitedly. "I understand. It's too big a deal."

"No, to the rehearsal. My hair color is off two shades, and I have to have it protein corrected tonight. And this is the only time I can have my eye liner tattooed."

"Oh." I was disappointed that she'd be there tomorrow. "Your liner tattooed? What's that?"

"They're all doing it in Paris. It hurts, but you never have to do it again."

What a totally superficial, narcissistic, selfish person she was. But I wished I had a little of that!

"Promise me you won't gasp when you see how I look at the wedding," she said.

Oh, God, I thought. She's going to do something to call attention to herself, like wear red when all the other bridesmaids are in black.

"Can't you give me a hint?" I asked.

"No, just be my friend no matter what."

Oh, boy. She was really trying to take over my day.

"I'm your friend no matter what," I said through clenched teeth.

When I put down the phone, suddenly I went into a panic. At my first wedding I had been oblivious to everything but sugar because I was scared of loving and letting myself be loved. This time I was scared of having everything. I had a perfect relationship, a perfect day, a perfect figure, in a perfect life. Was I worthy enough to have it all?

In OA they even say, "Nothing is going my way. Hooray." There's no excuse for going off your diet.

I called Jach and asked to speak to Lazaris.

"Lazaris, is this a dream? Am I really thin? Am I always going to be thin?"

"I was expecting your call tonight, Renée! How would you like to see that your fat body died? It was your last step."

"My body died?"

"Close your eyes. See yourself as a fat woman. Walk through a white crystal tunnel. See the light bounce off the rainbow prisms. Come out the underside of the tunnel to a mountaintop. Below is a huge green valley. Walk out to the side of the mountain. See yourself jumping off the bluff. The pun is intended. You were bluffing as a fat person. You were hiding behind your fat. Jump! The fat 'you' died. Now you're going to rebuild your body the way you wanted it to look. When you love how you look, open your eyes. See, you've regenerated yourself as slender as you wanted to be. You've become what you dreamed. You are thin. You are going to be thin. Most of all, you are *worthy to be thin.*"

Now I felt I had what was missing. The worthiness. I was prepared for my second wedding day. Well, almost.

All the guests were there on time. The ones I invited because I knew them and the ones I invited whom I didn't know but had always wanted to, like Esther Williams. She came and said, "I heard about you two and I admire you. Fernando would have liked to have shared this kind of a day with me. That's why I came."

Shelley Winters said, "It's nice to see someone married twenty years to the same person. I spent sixteen with three different men."

Joan Collins said, "When I see how happy you are, I'm inspired to get married again." (Three months later she did and invited us. I was very flattered. She copied my black-and-white wedding, only she was in light black and the groom was in white.)

Jane Fonda said, "This makes me want to renew my vows with Tom. I realize how much I love him today."

Burt Reynolds said, "I'm going to get married this year."

Barbra Streisand said, "What do you think of the guy I'm with? Should I do it?"

The head of the studio who once fired me said, "Renée, how'd you like to replace an actress I have to get rid of in London in a week?"

It was so great to tell him, "I can't. I have to finish my book. I'm behind schedule."

My ex-agent said, "Renée, did I just hear you turn down a movie?"

"Thank God," I said. "My life is my career."

To my amazement, Jach came to my wedding and brought Peny. I felt the ray of light that was Lazaris flittering everywhere. Lazaris is so joyous. It's not so hard to believe he's a Celestial Being after all.

Who do you think kept us waiting for the ceremony to

begin? You guessed it. The Other Woman came waddling in, fat as a hippo. Everyone gasped. I started to say something, but I remembered that she asked me not to. I kissed her and said nothing.

"Aren't you going to ask me what happened?" She did her French pout.

"What happened to what?" I pretended not to know what she was talking about.

"My figure! I went to have the fat sucked out of my body at a salon that uses a Japanese technique to melt the cellulite in your body and suck it out through a vacuum. I didn't know the diet they prescribed to rid yourself of toxins was mandatory or I would never have gone on my candy week."

"What's your candy week?"

"I suck a lollipop for eleven minutes before each meal to lose my appetite."

The Other Woman's Candy Diet

Breakfast 10:30 A.M.:	Suck a lollipop for eleven minutes before eating
	Scrambled eggs and toast
Lunch 4:00 P.M.:	Suck a lollipop for eleven minutes before eating
	Hamburger
Dinner 10:00 P.M.:	Suck a lollipop for eleven minutes before eating
	Roast Beef

(25 calories a lollipop)

"On the third day I indulged myself with an all-day dietetic sucker, and it triggered a chemical reaction in my body that caused a saccharin overdose, and I blew up like a balloon."

"How did you get the courage to come today, with all of Hollywood thinking of you as a sex symbol?" I tried not to gloat.

"Screw them. I binged before, I threw up before, I starved before, I binged before. So, I'll do it again tomorrow," she said in her inimitable French snarl. The real secret of her weight control was bulimia.

Maybe it's true that whenever someone loses, someone gains your loss. Matter has to go somewhere on the planet.

Anyway, whoever said revenge is sweet was mistaken in this case. When I saw her practically rolling downhill into my wedding party on that beautiful August afternoon, I felt pity for her. I was toned up, at my best weight, 115 pounds, and she was all swollen and muscle-bound, weighing in at at least 165.

She came to my wedding to steal the show one way or another, positive attention or negative attention.

"Tell me the truth. You had plastic surgery, didn't you?" the Other Woman asked me just before I walked down the aisle.

"No. What a wonderful compliment."

"Then what did you do to yourself? Your body is so perfect."

"It's my seven-course meal in a week Taylor-Made Diet." I pressed a copy of the diet and instructions into her hand.

"It looks too simple."

"It works, but you must keep saying 'I am what I'm going to be, thin.'"

It was incredible that I was telling this once svelte now obese Other Woman how to take charge of her life with my lifetime eating plan.

"You can feel yourself going from fat and stupid to thin and real as you eat your way into awareness," I said.

"I'll do it."

"Call me anytime. I'm happy to be your food sponsor."

Just then, the organ started playing Jewish folk music, and Joe and I danced down the aisle separately and circled each other, symbolizing separateness yet togetherness.

Five hundred guests attended, and you might think that I was gloating about getting revenge on some of them, but I was just happy they came. The head of the studio who didn't invite me to his party, the head of the network who fired me, the agent who didn't want to represent me, even the executive producer who had me dismissed years before. I've just replaced him as producer on a network show and found a new home base as president of the Taylor-Bologna Production Company. Our first project is a television special for Burt Reynolds that I'm directing. It made me giddy to think Joe and I were getting married again by Rabbi Cutler in Hollywood, which everyone thinks is a cynical town.

Rabbi Cutler said, "I haven't seen so many Italians wearing yarmulkes since Bugsy Siegel's wedding."

At the end of the ceremony Joe and I exchanged vows. "Renée, I've searched my heart for what to say to you today after twenty years, and what I wish for the next twenty is not more than what we've had together, but I can only hope for the same." Joe broke down in tears. "I love you," he cried.

Suddenly, I couldn't stop crying either. My mascara ran all over my face, making me look like a clown. "You're not going to believe this, Joe. I wrote the same thing to say to you. I don't need anything more. Usually I get so high being near a buffet table. You see, today's my pasta day. There are three great pastas here, and I only want a normal portion. I've been starving my whole life, but this afternoon I'm just happy to be accepted by my peers. And by myself too! I'm full without eating. My obsession has been lifted. Finally I have enough because I feel I *am* enough. I'm so grateful to all of you, for being in my life. I guess I'm where I always wanted to be. On 'maintenance.'"

P.S.

Right after our renewal ceremony, Joe and I had a honeymoon in Israel and Egypt. We took Gabriel along because it was such an incredible adventure. The Wailing Wall, the Dead Sea, visiting the pyramids and boating down the Nile. In one of the tombs in the Valley of Queens, I had the feeling I'd been there before and that I'd tasted the dates too.

"These dates grow only at this oasis," our camel driver said.

When I got back to the States I called Jach and talked to Lazaris.

"I've put off asking you about my past lives because I was too scared to find out. Now I do sense who I was but I want you to tell me what you know," I said.

"You lived in Egypt. You were a priestess who starved to death in the desert after ninety days at Aswân. You had already proved your holiness by going thirty-six hours in a coffin without eating. But the desert overcame you," Lazaris replied.

No wonder I was at home in the Valley of Queens and I recognized the dates. I must have died trying to find them.

"Is that why I see my life in terms of my diet? Is that why I'm a compulsive eater in this lifetime?"

"Yes. You also lived in Persia. Your mother took you to court when you were four because of your psychic powers. The king fed you until you weighed 300 pounds because he believed that the larger you were the more powerful you would be as a person."

"I still must hold those beliefs subconsciously—that large

is powerful and that there won't be enough food. How can I get over that?"

"Do the meditation where you fall through the opening in the cave, after walking along the ocean. Fall back to 4750 B.C. in Persia. Be with yourself at 300. Tell her to trust her gifts. She doesn't have to eat anymore."

"Does this mean that everyone who has a weight problem in this life had one in their last life?"

"They had some problem that relates to how they view themselves," Lazaris answered.

"What is the purpose of this lifetime for me on earth?"

"To let the miracle happen by helping people, by making them laugh at themselves."

My heart was beating fast. I realized it's no accident that my diet makes people laugh. Some people get hysterical when I describe what they get to eat and still lose.

"One more thing. Why didn't my mother appear to me at the Friars Club seánce in Hollywood? I was so disappointed."

"She's planning her next birth and she's very happy. This time she wants a musical career without the ancient harness that kept her frustrated and lacking confidence. She does look after you, though. You must be open to see all the little things she's attending to for you," Lazaris said.

Of course there's no way to prove to you that this is so. It doesn't matter. In my lifetime I am happy that in getting my own true body back on my Taylor-Made Diet, *I* am in control instead of the food. That's how I let the miracle happen.

12

THE TAYLOR-MADE DIET

Questions people ask me about my diet:

    Q: Will I have a nervous breakdown on your diet?
    A: Only if you were planning to have one anyway.

    Q: Will I stay with my husband on your diet?
    A: Better yours than mine.

    Q: How much longer will I live on your diet?
    A: Twelve hours and thirty-three minutes and two seconds.

    Q: Then, is it worth it to have only twelve hours and thirty-three minutes and two seconds longer on earth?
    A: Only if you are screwing.

    Q: How important is screwing in my life?
    A: One-third.

But seriously. I'm so happy with my new body and my new life that I wanted to help other people who, like me, have been diet junkies all their lives. Many of my friends and relatives have tried the Taylor-Made Diet, and everyone who does loses weight—I know you can too. Let me tell you why it works.

Our ancestors were hunters. When they found berries, they ate them all day. The next day they'd find a bear and eat it for three meals a day. One food a day was easier to absorb. They had no weight problems. It was a diet high in complex carbohydrates and low in fat, just like the Taylor-Made Diet. You'll see—you won't want to go off and binge because you are already bingeing three times a day at mealtimes!

You will lose 6 to 8 pounds the first week if you follow the diet to the letter, 3 to 5 pounds the second, and 2 to 4 pounds the third. After that, you can start all over with the program for the first week again, and you can lose 1 pound a week until you make your total weight loss.

I designed the diet to begin on a Tuesday, because nobody likes to start anything on a Monday. The rules are very simple. You may eat only three meals a day, nothing in between. At those meals you must eat the type of food described in the schedule below, but you can eat *as much of it as you like.* Stretch it out. You must take at least twenty relaxed minutes, but you can take longer. Eat slowly, chew, appreciate and enjoy. And with each bite, imagine your new, thin body. Believe me, you won't feel deprived!

Week One

TUESDAY:	FRUIT—EAT AS SUGGESTED.
WEDNESDAY:	GRAIN—EAT AS SUGGESTED.
THURSDAY:	SALAD WITH DRESSING—COMBINATION AS SUGGESTED.
FRIDAY:	FOWL
SATURDAY:	VEGETABLES—AS SUGGESTED, HOT OR COLD.
SUNDAY:	EGGS, ANY STYLE; FISH OR SHELLFISH AND MEAT, SAUTÉED, OR BROILED, PREPARED AS YOU LIKE THEM.
MONDAY:	ANY SWEET DESSERT. IF YOU CHOOSE ICE CREAM, DON'T EAT MORE THAN ONE PINT AT ONE MEAL.

Week Two

Tuesday:	Eggs and meat
Wednesday:	Salad
Thursday:	Fish
Friday:	Fruit
Saturday:	Grain
Sunday:	Vegetables
Monday:	Dessert

Week Three

Tuesday:	Meat
Wednesday:	Salad
Thursday:	Chicken or eggs, and fish
Friday:	Fruit
Saturday:	Grain
Sunday:	Vegetables
Monday:	Dessert

On the next few pages I have included the diet meal plan, one that I used with great success, to give you an idea of how to plan a menu. I strongly recommend that you do make a plan in advance and follow it exactly.

If I have suggested ingredients that you absolutely *hate* or are allergic to, you may delete them. Do not, under any circumstances, add ingredients that aren't listed. You might add something that doesn't combine properly, and it will add fat, not joy.

After three weeks you can rotate the diet back to the first week. I was always happiest on a diet when I had something to look forward to. With this plan, after your fruit day you can look forward to pasta, and when you get to your vegetables day, dessert comes next.

If you have special problems with food allergies, here are some suggestions:

FIRST WEEK

	BREAKFAST	LUNCH	DINNER
Tuesday (Fruit)	Fresh pineapple	Apples	Dried fruit medley: raisins, apricots, figs and prunes (no preservatives)
Wednesday (Grain)	Two bagels with butter or sour cream (no cream cheese)	Macaroni with butter and parsley	Fried rice made with sesame oil, garlic, ginger, broccoli, onions and peas
Thursday (Salad)	Hearts of lettuce and sliced tomatoes with sour cream and fresh garlic or oil and vinegar	Mixed green salad with oil and vinegar	Raw carrots, broccoli, zucchini, radishes, with garlic or sour cream, dill and curry dip
Friday (Fowl)	Cold turkey leg-wing	Cold roast or broiled chicken	Chicken, any style
Saturday (Vegetables)	Cooked vegetables, any three	Baked potato, any style	Eggplant and tomatoes with sautéed onions
Sunday (Fowl, Eggs, Fish, Meat)	Eggs, as you like them	Fish, any style (seafood included)	Roast beef
Monday (Dessert)	Coffee cake of choice, or baked apples with cinnamon	Brownies or pears	One pint of ice cream, or canteloupe

SECOND WEEK

	BREAKFAST	LUNCH	DINNER
Tuesday (Eggs and meat)	Two scrambled eggs, any style, or hamburger, or combination (or steak all day)	Meat, lamb or veal, broiled	Steak
Wednesday (Salad)	Lettuce, tomato and onion salad with dressing (sour cream or oil and vinegar)	Endive and watercress with oil and vinegar; or mushroom and spinach salad	Cold Chinese salad made with sesame oil, rice vinegar and bean sprouts and ginger; coleslaw made with red and green cabbage, carrots and onions
Thursday (Fish)	Crab, tuna or salmon, or fish cakes	Fish, any kind; baked, sautéed or broiled	Seafood buffet: shrimp, lobster, oysters, smoked fish, caviar
Friday (Fruit)	Fruit: Prunes	Fresh strawberries	Three baked bananas
Saturday (Grain)	Renée Risotto: instant rice, mushrooms and onions, sautéed	Spaghetti with olive oil and garlic	Penne arrabbiate: noodles, tomato, garlic, olives, hot red peppers
Sunday (Vegetables)	Ménage à trois: mixed sautéed squash—yellow, button, zucchini	Hot or cold: string beans and mushrooms	Baked potato, asparagus, spinach sautéed with olive oil
Monday (Dessert)	Danish or dried apricots	Cake or cookies of choice, or pineapple	Natural ice cream (one pint of Häagen-Dazs) or bananas

THIRD WEEK

	BREAKFAST	LUNCH	DINNER
Tuesday (Meat)	Sautéed veal or hamburger patty	Beef ribs, barbecued or plain, or any meat of choice	Steak
Wednesday (Salad)	Three lettuces, mixed, with oil and vinegar	Coleslaw	Scallions, beets, spinach, radishes, watercress, parsley, endive, leeks, carrots and mushrooms
Thursday (Chicken or eggs, fish)	Cold chicken, or eggs, any style	Tuna fish	Broiled fish of choice
Friday (Fruit)	Melon balls: honeydew, cantaloupe and watermelon	Mixed tropical fruit: pineapple, papaya and kiwi	Berries: raspberries, strawberries and blueberries
Saturday (Grain)	Cold pasta salad with oil, garlic and basil	Spaghetti with tomatoes and basil	Spaghetti primavera: made with broccoli, peas, tomato, zucchini, light cream (not milk), oil and garlic
Sunday (Vegetables)	Hot or cold artichoke with vinaigrette dressing, or corn on the cob	Two baked or boiled potatoes	Vegetable tempura; or stir-fried vegetables with sesame oil, garlic and ginger; or steamed vegetables
Monday (Dessert)	Glazed donuts, or mixed berries, fresh or frozen	Chocolate chip cookies or raisins	Ice cream, or baked or raw apples and pears

- If you are a vegetarian, substitute your usual protein source, including cheese and nuts, for the animal proteins.
- If you are allergic to sugar, make your cake with fruit juices or fructose or maltose.
- If you are allergic to milk, have tofu ice cream or nondairy sherbet.
- If you are allergic to wheat, try artichoke or spinach pasta instead (available at health food stores).
- If you are allergic to eggs, have protein of your choice.

If you want to lose weight very quickly, order and prepare your food salt free and eliminate diet sodas. Here's a slight variation of the meal plan that will make it happen faster:

- Start your pasta day with fruit.
- Start your meat and fish days with fruit.
- On dessert day, eat fruit instead of dessert, at one or two or all the meals.

On any fruit day or any dessert day, you can substitute all watermelon or all grapes for the prescribed fruit. If you choose to do this, it is imperative that you stick to it or you'll bloat instead of lose.

My brother, Bernard, lost 15 pounds on the Taylor-Made Diet the first week, and 60 pounds total. He calls it his "forbidden fantasy" diet, because he has always wanted to eat pasta three times a day! My friend, Nancy, lost 8 pounds the first week and 30 pounds in total. What she loved about the Taylor-Made Diet was that she was never hungry because she ate as much as she wanted every day. My friend Milton lost 6 pounds the first week and 20 pounds in all. What he liked about the diet was that it satisfied his exotic tastes (he's a Chinese food nut).

If you commit yourself to abstinence except for three meals a day, I assure you that you'll find it easy to lose.

There's only one danger in going on my diet. It will work and you will have to deal with looking the best you ever have.

I wish I could be there with you, going through it day by day, but in a way I am. That's why I told you my story. I wanted to show how being fat was a distraction that kept me from dealing with the real issues of my life. Once I got thin, I found I had learned:

- To trust myself.
- Not to allow success in my career to have power over my happiness, instead of feeling my own personal power.
- Not to hurt myself if I had less than others (my envy was self-punishment).
- Life doesn't have to be a struggle—it's easy once I let myself receive all the love that was there for me.
- To feel gratitude for all I have, which is the cure for envy as well.
- To release my guilt for having a better life than my mother. Children are supposed to!

I hope you feel that if I could do it, so can you. Good luck. I've already done a meditation on you. You're already thin. You just have to claim it.